Tahitian
Transformation

Women and Change in the Developing World

Series Editor
Mary H. Moran, Colgate University

Editorial Board

Tahitian Transformation

Gender and Capitalist Development in a Rural Society

Victoria S. Lockwood

Lynne Rienner Publishers   •   Boulder & London

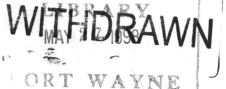
Published in the United States of America in 1993 by
Lynne Rienner Publishers, Inc.
1800 30th Street, Boulder, Colorado 80301

and in the United Kingdom by
Lynne Rienner Publishers, Inc.
3 Henrietta Street, Covent Garden, London WC2E 8LU

Library of Congress Cataloging-in-Publication Data
Lockwood, Victoria S., 1953–
   Tahitian transformation : gender and capitalist development in a
rural society / Victoria S. Lockwood.
    p. cm.—(Women and change in the developing world)
   Includes bibliographical references and index.
   ISBN 1-55587-317-0 (hc) ISBN 1-55587-391-X (pb)
   1. Rural development—Society Islands—Tahiti. 2. Tahiti—Rural
conditions. 3. Women in development—Society Islands—Tahiti.
I. Title. II. Series.
HN939.5.T34L625 1992
307.1'412'0996211—dc20
                                   92-24045
                                       CIP

British Cataloguing in Publication Data
A Cataloguing in Publication record for this book
is available from the British Library.

Printed and bound in the United States of America

This book is dedicated to John and Henry

Contents

Part 2 ▲ Rural Tahitian Society and Capitalism

▲

Illustrations

Photographs

Maps

Figure

Tables

▲

Acknowledgments

Since my research first began, in 1980, I have received the continuing help, support, and guidance of many friends, colleagues, and institutions. The first year of research (1980–1981) was partially funded by a Department of Anthropology, University of California/Los Angeles Travel Grant and by a University of California Regents Travel Grant. My doctoral committee at UCLA, Drs. Timothy Earle, Philip Newman, and Allen Johnson, helped me to plan and complete the initial research in French Polynesia. I would like to particularly thank Dr. Tim Earle for his support and guidance throughout my doctoral studies at UCLA. His research in Hawaii first interested me in working in Oceania, and his own rigorous standards of analysis in economic anthropology have served as a model for me and a standard I have tried to maintain.

In organizing the first period of fieldwork on Tubuai, I was helped enormously by Dr. Paula Levin. She conducted research on the island in the mid-1970s and used her contacts to help me become established on the island and to find a place to live that first year. Since then, she has been a friend who has offered unqualified encouragement.

I am grateful to Smith College for the Culpeper Postdoctoral Fellowship, which I was privileged to receive in 1984–1985. During that year I was able to analyze the early Tubuai data and to prepare a research proposal to return to French Polynesia.

The second major phase of research took place in 1985 and then again in 1987; it was funded by a grant from the Anthropology Program, National Science Foundation (#BNS 8507861), which I gratefully acknowledge. Research in French Polynesia in 1991 was supported by a University Research Council Faculty Seed Grant, Southern Methodist University. I would like to thank Provost Ruth Morgan (SMU) for her support of this program.

I have received help and support from many colleagues and government officials in Papeete. Most important, I would like to thank the Haut-Commissaire de la République en Polynésie Française for permission to conduct the research. I have benefited greatly from the support of researchers at the Office de la Recherche Scientifique et Technique, Outre-Mer (ORSTOM) in Papeete. They also most kindly made their library and government documents available to me. The former head of the Service de l'Économie Rurale in French Polynesia, Jean-Claude Reboul, also offered valuable advice and guidance, for which I am grateful.

On Tubuai, I have received an incredible amount of tireless cooperation and support from Saira Mateau, chef du service de l'Économie Rurale for the Austral Islands. Saira offered his time and expertise and opened many doors for me. I am most grateful for his willingness to teach me about Tubuai agriculture and for his friendship. In 1987, I was fortunate to be able to work with Olga Tanepau, agent for the territorial bureau of agriculture; her help was instrumental in interviewing a wide range of island cultivators, particularly the women farmers with whom she worked closely. I would also like to thank Philippe Paccou, head of the Société de Développement d'Agriculture et de la Pêche on Tubuai, for his help with information on the potato project.

It is not possible to name all of the many individuals and families on Tubuai who generously opened their doors and hearts to me over the years. I am most grateful for their friendship, hospitality, and willingness to include me in their lives. I would particularly like to thank Emilie Tehoiri and Charley Audouin, Ura Tehoiri, Toimata and Areti Mervin, Émile Teihotaata, Emma and Taunoa Tanepau, Florine Tahiata, Marie and Taro Utahia, Lynette and Taputuhurupee Taroatehaihai, Teina and Roo Mae, and Marcelle Tihoni.

The Department of Anthropology at Southern Methodist University has supported my research endeavors. I was fortunate to have two of its finest graduate students, Katherine Browne and Lance Rasbridge, work with me on Tubuai as assistants during the 1987 fieldwork.

I have benefited greatly from the comments and suggestions offered by colleagues who generously read parts or all of this manuscript. They include James Peoples, Robert Borofsky, Caroline Brettell, John Connell, Stephen Henningham, Christine Ward Gailey, and Mary Moran. Responsibility for errors or misstatements remains, however, my own.

I would like to thank my parents, Catherine and Warren Lockwood, for their unflagging support over many years. Finally, I dedicate this book to my husband and son, John and Henry Ubelaker.

V.S.L.

▲ 1

Introduction: The Architecture of the World System

As vast regions of the non-Western world were integrated into colonial empires during the eighteenth and nineteenth centuries, the European powers established an international division of labor between themselves and their subordinate colonies (Wallerstein 1974). In this unequal division, the rapidly industrializing European nations extracted wealth (resources and labor) from the non-Western societies under their control. As capitalist relations of production penetrated non-Western societies, one integrated "capitalist world system" emerged. Economically and politically subordinate to the industrialized nations at the core of this system, the less technologically developed and largely impoverished non-Western societies stagnated on the periphery.

This compelling world system macromodel, described in detail by Wallerstein (1974) and others (see Worsley 1984), has provided important insights into the structure of both colonial era and contemporary world political/economic relations. But like most macromodels, it largely ignores variability in the small-scale, local-level processes that constitute the system as a whole (Mintz 1977). The world system model, for example, pays little attention to the highly variable ways in which individual communities were (and are) integrated into the larger world system. In other words, it largely ignores the diverse ways in which capitalism has expanded around the globe, as well as the multiple forms capitalist exploitation can take. Moreover, the model pays little attention to the many diverse ways in which the peoples of the non-Western world have responded to their incorporation into market economies and to their domination by the West.

This variability in local-level processes has several sources. In their contacts with non-Western societies, Europeans sought different types of resources (land, labor, various commodities) in different places (see Lingenfelter 1977). They also chose to interact with indigenous populations in different ways (see Mintz 1977; Nash 1981). At the same time, culturally diverse indigenous peoples' responses to Westernization and capitalism have ranged from accommodation to resistance to rejection. The nature of native

1

peoples' responses has played a major role—one that tends to be underestimated—in shaping the impact of capitalism on their lives.

The impact of capitalism on non-Western societies has varied greatly. In some societies, indigenous institutions and cultural patterns have been replaced by Western institutions, while in others "traditional" institutions and practices remain in place today. In some, capitalist relations of production have replaced indigenous economic patterns, while in others a "peasant" mode of production, which articulates capitalist and precapitalist relations of production, dominates rural economies. Some indigenous populations are today rapidly moving toward "Westernization," while others reject it and seek their own path.

Recognizing the great diversity in how capitalism has expanded around the globe, Marcus and Fisher (1986:80) suggest: "These processes are more complex than the dominant paradigms seem able to represent them, and thus one obvious course is for political economy to rebuild understandings of macrolevel systems from the bottom up." They go on to advocate that scholars place less emphasis on the world "system," and instead focus "their attention on close analyses of the historic and ethnographic conditions of regions and locales" (1986:81).

Whether or not one follows the much-debated "interpretivist" approach of Marcus and Fisher (1986), the potential benefits of studying the world system from the bottom up—by analyzing the conditions of particular cases—are clear. Instead of forcing different regions' diverse experiences with capitalism into one overworked and inadequate world system macromodel, researchers can instead acknowledge and highlight the variety of ways capitalism has taken root in culturally and environmentally diverse locales. And instead of homogenizing the experiences of one undifferentiated category of all native people under Western domination, researchers can more appropriately highlight the many creative strategies culturally diverse native peoples have adopted to deal with that domination.

By dissecting individual cases in their historically particularistic way, anthropologists have made an important contribution to understanding the underlying architecture of the world system (Mintz 1977:255). It is my goal in this study to analyze some of the variability in this architecture by examining the relatively atypical case of one region of the world, France's overseas territory of French Polynesia. In so doing, I describe the particular transformation capitalism has wrought on rural Tahitian society and on the lives of Tahitian men and women.

▲ France's Overseas Territory of French Polynesia

French Polynesia, a colony (and now territory) of France since the 1800s, is made up of the five major island groups clustered around Tahiti and its port,

Papeete (see Map 1.1). These groups include the Society Islands (Îles Sous-le-Vent, Îles du Vent), the Austral Islands, the Tuamotus, and the Marquesas. The territory covers 4 million square kilometers of the southeastern Pacific Ocean, encompassing over 120 islands (many uninhabited)—some volcanic and others low-lying coral atolls. Today, the population of the islands—about 190,000 people—is culturally pluralistic; it is approximately 70 percent Tahitian, 10 percent French, 8 percent Chinese, and 12 percent persons of mixed French/Tahitian heritage (or *demi*).

Long romanticized as a tropical paradise of white sand beaches, coconut trees, and gentle natives, the islands have attracted sailors, beachcombers, and reclusive artists since their discovery by the Western world. More recently, Western tourists have sought them out as an idyllic retreat far from the fast pace of urban life.

While the Tahitian islands' tropical paradise mystique is well known, the hard realities faced by this French territory today are not. Little-known facts of its contemporary situation include the territory's continuing status as a French possession and home of France's controversial nuclear testing installations; its stagnant, underdeveloped, and resource-poor economy, which is heavily dependent on French aid; and its rapidly growing population locked between two competing worlds and two identities: one French, dominant, and "civilized," the other Tahitian, subordinate, and *sauvage*. Like many other less-developed regions of the Third World long under foreign domination, this tropical paradise is today struggling to find its own identity and to deal with severe economic and social problems.

While islanders have recently been granted some local self-government (*autonomie interne*), they remain the territorial subjects of France. Unlike other Western powers who have participated in Third World decolonization since World War II, France has determinedly fought the loss of its colonies (e.g., Indochina and Algeria). Today it retains a far-flung network of eleven colonial outposts, mostly islands scattered in every ocean of the world (Aldrich and Connell 1988). France's holdings have been described as the "only surviving colonial empire of worldwide dimensions" (Chesneaux 1986). They include New Caledonia, French Polynesia, and the tiny islands of Wallis and Futuna in the Pacific; French Guyana in South America; Martinique and Guadeloupe in the Caribbean; and various other small islands in the Indian Ocean and off the coast of Newfoundland. These outposts are generally of little economic value (with the exception of nickel-producing New Caledonia), yet they permit France to achieve a military/strategic presence in global affairs. France considers this politically motivated presence to be essential to its security and to its status as an international power (Chesneaux 1986; Aldrich and Connell 1989; Henningham 1989a). Military installations located in France's overseas possessions include nuclear testing facilities and

Map 1.1 French Polynesia

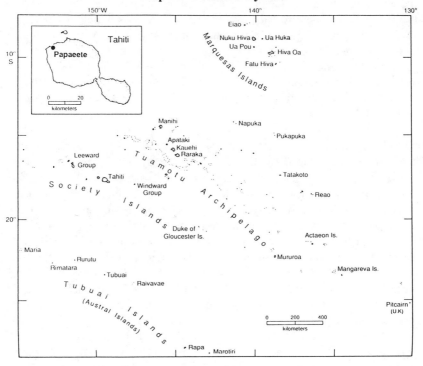

Source: Fairbairn, T. I. J., et al. *The Pacific Islands: Politics, Economics, and International Relations.* Honolulu: International Relations Program and Pacific Islands Development Program at the East-West Center, 1991. Reprinted with permission.

military bases in French Polynesia, and a missile and space station in French Guyana.

Political and Economic Integration

In the postdecolonization era, France cements ties to its foreign possessions by administratively integrating them into the French state and by implementing a financially benevolent form of neocolonialism called "welfare state colonialism" (Bertram and Watters 1985). The critical element in welfare state colonialism is the constant reinforcing of economic dependency on the state. Dependency is generated by providing local populations with numerous social welfare and development programs (including government salaries), which generate an artificially high standard of living. These relatively affluent populations realize that they would be unable to achieve this standard of living on their own.

Today, for example, the Tahitian population—French citizens—possesses one of the highest standards of living of any island society in the Pacific. It is a standard of living that rivals that found in many of the developed, industrialized nations. For example, the average annual familial income on the island of Tubuai, a rapidly developing rural outer island, was $12,000 a year in the late 1980s. Yet, beneath this veneer of prosperity lies a highly dependent and economically marginal society. Without French aid, subsidies, government salaries, and various other transfer payments, the Tahitian islands would assume the status of an impoverished colonial backwater.

In recent decades, various development programs aimed at promoting regional and world market production (exports) in the islands of French Polynesia have been an important feature of welfare state colonialism there. Under the auspices of these programs and with the help of large subsidies, some Tahitian smallholders produce copra and vanilla for international markets. In the Tuamotu atolls, several small cooperatives run by islanders (and some by large Japanese firms) harvest black pearls for international markets. A few islands used to export small quantities of coffee to world markets, but output has shrunk and most is now consumed within the region. Other islands produce European vegetables or fruits for the expanding regional market (as substitutes for foreign imports).

With their high incomes, rural Tahitians also participate in the world market economy as consumers of manufactured and luxury goods produced in the industrialized nations of the West and Far East (Japan, Taiwan). Through Papeete, rural Tahitians have access to and purchase virtually every consumer and luxury good available in the industrialized nations, including state-of-the-art electronics and late-model automobiles and trucks.

In many ways, then, Tahitian islanders' integration into the world system differs from that of other less developed Third World societies. While the latter are frequently characterized by poverty and underdevelopment, rural Tahitian communities are relatively affluent and have access to well-paying government jobs, welfare payments, and heavily subsidized "development" programs.

But the islands are like other regions of the Third World in that capitalist relations of production have increasingly penetrated rural Tahitian society as commodity production and wage labor have been introduced. Consequently, commodity production now dominates rural island economies that only thirty years ago were focused on traditional subsistence agriculture (taro and tree crops) and fishing.

Despite important differences in structural context, the impact of capitalism on rural Tahitian communities has been similar in some critical ways to its impact on other regions of the non-Western world. Yet, there have also been important differences. Assessing these major similarities and differences is the aim of this case study.

The Rural Island of Tubuai

The focus of the analysis is rural Tahitian society, specifically the small outer island of Tubuai (see Map 1.2). Even though remotely located in the southerly Austral Islands[1] (700 kilometers due south of Tahiti), Tubuai has experienced the full brunt of French-style Westernization and welfare state colonialism. In particular, it has been a major target of government-sponsored development programs since the early 1960s. Consequently, in 1991, Tahitians on neighboring islands described Tubuai as more *évolue* (developed, evolved) than their own communities.

What other Tahitian islanders mean by *évolue* is that Tubuaians are well integrated into the regional capitalist economy and that their material lifestyle is significantly Westernized. Tubuaians have access both to government jobs and government-sponsored projects that promote commercial agriculture (potatoes and other European vegetables) and commodity exports. In addition, Tubuaians have adopted Western-style consumerism; many islanders own television sets, Sony stereos, and Peugeot or Mitsubishi trucks. The island's population of about 2,000 is not only well integrated into regional and world markets, but its outlook on world affairs is increasingly cosmopolitan. Although concerned with local island affairs, Tubuaians often turn their attention to major events taking place in Papeete and Paris, recognizing these events' potential impact on their own lives.

I began research on Tubuai in 1980–1981, first studying rural Tahitians' responses to the French/territorial government's agricultural development programs (Joralemon 1983a). At various times over the next decade (1985, 1987, 1991), I returned to Tubuai to follow up on the early research and to document the impact of rapid Westernization and capitalist integration on island society. I was particularly interested in the structural changes that

Map 1.2 Island of Tubuai

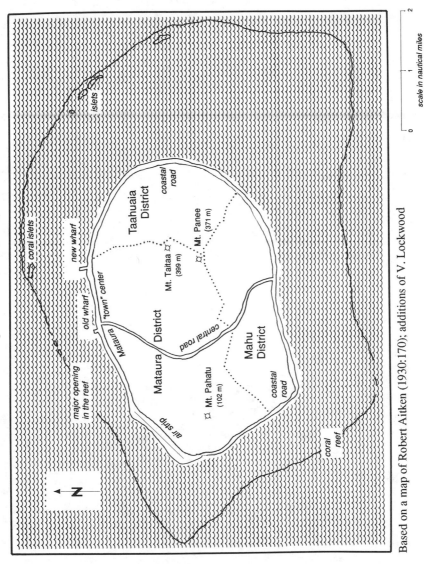

Based on a map of Robert Aitken (1930:170); additions of V. Lockwood

Tubuai beach and lagoon (photo: Lockwood)

Tubuai's interior mountains (photo: Lockwood)

One family's traditional fare ni'au *house, with their pickup truck parked in front* (photo: Lockwood)

Tubuai women have assumed roles unprecedented in rural Tahitian society (photo: Lockwood).

would accompany the greater penetration of capitalist relations of production, and in how islanders were interacting with and responding to capitalism. As the study progressed, I came to realize that one of the major arenas in which development-related change was taking place was in gender relations.

In Tubuai's development decades of the 1960s, 1970s, and 1980s, the French government, pursuing its own political agendas, had created many of the structural linkages that would enable this previously isolated and remote outer-island society to participate in regional and world markets. The government had also fully integrated islanders into the French welfare state and promoted their financial dependence on it.

When the study began, in the early 1980s, I did not anticipate the evolutionary course capitalist development would take on Tubuai. In the early 1980s, it appeared that Tubuai was well on its way to local-level capitalism. Large-scale commercial farmers of potatoes—the new government-sponsored cash crop—were concentrating wealth as well as control over familially owned land (within the traditionally derived, kin-based land tenure system) (Joralemon 1986). The successes of this expansion-oriented, highly entrepreneurial group of farmers appeared at the time to foreshadow the evolution of structural changes (in land tenure and so on) commensurate with the growth of large-scale capitalist agriculture on the island.

By the late 1980s, however, this transformation had not occurred. Indeed, large-scale capitalist farming had mostly failed, while small-scale, household-based production had been reinforced. In spite of the new and lucrative development opportunities in commodity production, Tubuai households had not shifted their resources fully into market production but maintained subsistence production. And instead of a trend toward individualization of landholding (private property), joint (collective) ownership of land remained strongly entrenched. In other words, market integration and capitalism were reinforcing a peasant mode of production in which capitalist and noncapitalist relations of production were articulated.

Thus, despite welfare state colonialism and islanders' affluence, Tubuaians' interaction with capitalism was generating the same socio-economic pattern that had been identified elsewhere in the Third World: the peasant mode of production. Market integration had not brought local-level capitalism to the islands as some scholars might have predicted.

Nor did I anticipate the unprecedented roles Tubuai women would take on in commercial potato farming. According to the precepts of rural Tahitian society, men are the farmers and women take care of the household and children. Nevertheless, by 1991 almost half (43 percent) of all potato farmers were women. Whereas in most documented cases, Third World women are notable nonparticipants in introduced, Western-style agricultural development programs (even where they play major roles in indigenous agriculture), Tubuai women were swamping the potato cultivation project.

Women's development participation, as well as their ownership of important agricultural lands (the means of production) within the familial system, raised important questions about exactly how island women were interacting with capitalism. It also raised important questions about how capitalism was affecting women's generally subordinate position in rural Tahitian society, as well as overall patterns of gender stratification.

▲ Goals and Organization of the Study

In this study, my goal is to bridge the gap that separates a macrolevel analysis of territorial/French/world political-economic interactions from a microlevel analysis of the lives of rural Tahitian islanders impinged upon and shaped by those interactions. These two levels become one integrated system—a subsection of the world system—by a two-way flow of resources between Tahitian communities and France.

That flow is regulated by the set of structural linkages (administrative ties, market ties, and so on) that integrate islanders into regional and world markets, the French state, and Western culture. To understand the nature of these linkages and how they affect islanders' lives, one must appreciate the operating agendas of the French state that created them. But one must also appreciate the operating agendas of islanders themselves, for these agendas dictate the highly variable ways in which islanders choose to participate (or not participate) in the linkages available to them.

Throughout this analysis, I adopt a historical perspective—a perspective that is critical to understanding the path along which Tahitian society has evolved since its first contact with the West. Only by following that path can one gain insights into the nature of the forces that have shaped contemporary Tahitian society.

But whether discussing the colonial era or the contemporary era, the macrolevel or the microlevel, a consistent theme throughout the study is a critique of capitalism's impact on non-Western societies. As capitalism promotes structural change in rural communities, one cannot avoid reflecting on whether the situation of those communities has improved or deteriorated as a result. The answers are never black and white.

Part 1: The Historical-Structural
Context of Contemporary Tahitian Society

In Part 1, I analyze the transformation of Tahitian society that took place during the colonial era. In Chapter 2, I describe how Tahitian society responded to Western contact and then how French colonial officials and

Christian missionaries set out to change and "civilize" it. I also discuss how islanders were drawn into a dependent, colonial export economy and began producing commodities—mainly copra and vanilla for world markets.

Chapter 3 is devoted specifically to examining how Tahitian women were affected by the many changes that took place during these years of Westernizing transformation. As capitalist relations of production penetrated rural economies, these structural relations were replicated within the major unit of economic production, the Tahitian household. This altered precontact patterns of gender stratification and established the conditions for women's relative subordination in the contemporary Neo-Tahitian household and community.

In Chapter 4, I follow rural Tahitian society into the modern era, tracing the evolution of French political agendas for its territory from the 1800s to the post–World War II Cold War era. In response to Cold War politics, France built nuclear testing installations in the Tahitian islands in the early 1960s, severely disrupting the regional economy while promoting massive regional economic growth. At the same time, France sought to engender the Tahitian population's goodwill to its ongoing neocolonial presence by interacting with it in a new way—through welfare state colonialism.

Part 2: Rural Tahitian Society and Capitalism

In Part 2, I shift from a historical perspective on the macrolevel political-economic context of the French territory to a contemporary focus on the microlevel of rural communities. I look specifically at how the outer-island society of Tubuai has been affected by the rapid development and greater market integration of the last three decades.

In Chapter 5, I examine the various structural linkages that now tie Tubuai economically, politically, socially, and culturally to the regional capital of Papeete, to France, and to the world. I also look specifically at how Tubuai men and women participate in those linkages.

In Chapter 6, I analyze the failure of these linkages to sustain a transition within Tubuai society to local-level capitalism. Instead, the peasant mode of production (which reflects the activities of "commodity producing peasant households"—see Cook 1982) prevails as the dominant mode of production. The form this mode of production takes in rural Tahitian society is described.

In Chapter 7, I look at how islanders have interacted with capitalism by tracing the evolution of their variable participation in the potato cultivation project. This analysis highlights the internal heterogeneity of the Tubuai community, a heterogeneity created by generational, gender, and socioeconomic differences. Because individuals and families differ and possess different goals, they choose diverse strategies for fulfilling their needs within the peasant mode of production. By isolating the factors that shape islanders' economic behavior, one also gains insights into the various internal forces responsible for reinforcing the stability and viability of Tubuai's peasant mode of production.

In Chapter 8, I look at the important transformation in contemporary women's roles brought about by potato development and Westernization. I then examine what impact women's independent potato cultivation and increasing financial autonomy may have on their subordinate status in the household and on prevailing patterns of gender stratification. Finally, I consider what general impact capitalism may have on women if the peasant mode of production gives way to a fuller penetration of capitalist relations of production in rural Tahitian society.

In Chapter 9, "Scenarios for the Future," I speculate upon what the present trajectory of modernizing change may mean for the futures of rural Tahitian men and women.

▲ Note

1. Anthropological sources on the Austral Islands include Hanson 1970; Marshall 1961; Panoff 1970; Buton 1974; Ravault 1979; Perrin 1978; Cook 1976; Levin 1978; Aitken 1930; Tercinier 1962; Verin 1964.

PART 1

The Structural-Historical Context of Contemporary Tahitian Society

▲ 2
The Forces of Transformation

The centuries of French colonial domination and missionary indoctrination that followed the European discovery of the Tahitian islands have left an indelible imprint on them. Each of these forces has played a powerful role in shaping the postcontact transformation of Tahitian society, as well as in creating modern Tahitian society. While Tahitian islanders' responses to the forces impinging upon them have played an important role in these processes, the overall direction of change has consistently reflected the priorities of a Western world bent on sociopolitical domination, capitalist incorporation, and religious conversion.

Like so many contemporary Third World peoples colonized centuries ago, Tahitians today know little of their ancient heritage or of the highly stratified, warlike chiefdoms their ancestors first fashioned when the islands were initially settled about 1,000 years ago. Contemporary islanders see themselves as a people who share in many French institutions and customs, indeed who are French citizens, yet who belong to the islands and are intrinsically *ta'ata Tahiti* (Tahitians). Proud of that cultural identity, they maintain a certain distance from the imposing world of French civilization around them. At the same time, that dominant world keeps them at a distance, for in the eyes of the outsiders, the Tahitians' closeness to the earth and the ocean, and their uniquely Tahitian ways of viewing the world, taint them with a certain "savageness" that even years of French schooling cannot erase.

To understand the transformation of Tahitian society, one must first look to the islands' ancient heritage and precontact roots, for the "transformation has been less than total" (Campbell 1989:226). Although deeply buried, these roots underpin a number of important contemporary institutions, including land tenure, kinship, and agricultural practices. They also continue to be an active component of contemporary Tahitian worldview.

▲ Precontact Tahitian Society

Of all of the regions of the world, the islands of the Pacific were the last to be discovered and settled by human populations. Archaeological and linguistic data suggest that the ancestors of the early Polynesians probably migrated from eastern Indonesia, settling the western Melanesian islands by 2,000 B.C., and then moving out into the islands of western Polynesia (Fiji, Samoa, and Tonga) about 1500 B.C. (Bellwood 1987). The major islands of eastern Polynesia (the Marquesas, Society Islands, and the Hawaiian Islands) were subsequently settled probably between 200 B.C. and A.D. 700.

Although the islands that dot the Pacific are separated by "empty and perilous" expanses of ocean (Oliver 1974), the early Polynesians were excellent navigators and adept sailors. In making their way from island to island, they navigated by the sun, stars, and ocean currents. Although the discovery of some islands may have been accidental, the settling of most was in all likelihood intentional. Conditions of resource scarcity and chronic warfare forced some groups to leave and search for new island homelands. Setting out in canoes to find land over the horizon, they carried with them the basic essentials they would need to make a new life: staple crops (taro, breadfruit, bananas, coconuts), livestock (pigs), and stone tools.

The peoples who came to settle what would become the Polynesian culture area—the islands encompassed by the triangle formed by Hawaii, New Zealand, and Easter Island—shared a common ancestral heritage, similar subsistence adaptations to island environments, and a "Polynesian" cultural configuration. They made their living by cultivating root and tree crops and by exploiting the rich lagoon and ocean resources around them. Although there was variation in Polynesian social systems, particularly between those of relatively rich volcanic islands and resource-poor atolls (see Sahlins 1958), Polynesian societies were generally organized into stratified chiefdoms. Kinship served as the central principle articulating social, economic, and political affairs.

While some of the more remote islands remained isolated from others after settlement, it was common for islands located near others or in the same group to be loosely affiliated either politically or through exchange, and occasionally through elite intermarriages. Before Europeans interfered in local political affairs, however, consolidated political units larger than a single island were rare. Even in the relatively clustered Society Islands, whose precontact population probably exceeded 45,000 people (Goldman 1970:170 estimates 200,000), most islands were fragmented into independent political units; the main island of Tahiti itself was territorially divided into six mutually hostile and competitive chiefdoms at contact (Bellwood 1987). There is, however, evidence suggesting that some of the smaller atolls of the neighboring northwestern Tuamotus paid tribute to chiefdoms on Tahiti

(Bellwood 1987:84), and that Tahiti regularly exchanged surplus foods with its neighboring Society Islands (Maude 1959).

For the most part, however, the islands that would become politically consolidated in the colonial era as French Polynesia (the Societies, Tuamotus, Australs, Marquesas, and Gambiers) were separate political and social entities prior to contact. In the more remote groups like the Australs and Marquesas, linguistic divergence and the development of unique cultural traits were evidence of their relative isolation from other islands.

Thus the term "Tahitian," used today to describe islanders of all five groups of French Polynesia, reflects modern political reality as opposed to actual cultural identity. Douglas Oliver, renowned scholar of Pacific island societies, uses the term "Maohi" to refer to the indigenous inhabitants of the Society Islands, reserving the term "Tahitian" to refer to the inhabitants of Tahiti itself. "Maohi" was the term used by indigenous Society Islanders to refer to themselves; eventually its usage was extended to other nearby islanders (Oliver 1974:6). To describe the general cultural patterns shared by all of the island groups of the territory, I use the term "Maohi" to refer to the ancestors of all contemporary "Tahitian" islanders, including the Marquesans, Tuamotuans, and Austral Islanders.

Maohi Society Before Contact

Ancient Maohi society, like the other major Polynesian societies (Hawaiian Islands, Tonga, Easter, and so on), was a highly stratified, class-structured social system in which one's relative rank was determined genealogically (Oliver 1974; Sahlins 1958; Goldman 1970). Because one's birth determined one's social status, classes were highly endogamous, and the elite frequently married close relatives.

A numerically small class of chiefs and their families, the *ari'i*, occupied the top rung of privilege and power. Below them were the *ra'atira*, the lesser chiefs and bureaucrats. The mass of the population, the commoners (*manahune*), occupied the lowest strata, being superior only to a contingent of slaves and war captives.

Maohi chiefs acquired their position through a system of primogeniture, although status rivalries and political intrigues over relative rank (and chiefly succession) were common (Goldman 1970). First-born offspring of first-born offspring (male or female) possessed more *mana,* supernatural power/ efficacy, than the lesser-born and thus greater "divine sanctity." Goldman (1970:182, citing Henry 1928:229) notes that "the highest chiefs were descendants of the high gods and were entitled to wear the feather girdle, the costume of the gods. They carried the *mana* of the people." Thus, politics and religion were closely interwoven, forming one all-encompassing social system of which "religion was the keystone" (see Hanson 1973:2).

One of the chief's most critical roles was to interact with the supernatural as high priest, offering prayers and sacrifices to a pantheon of gods and goddesses, local (territorial/occupational) spirits, and ancestral spirits. In so doing, he sustained the spiritual vitality of the community. A specialized class of priests oversaw the religious paraphernalia and organized ceremonies at the group's *marae,* the sacred stone platform where rituals and sacrifices were performed.

Extended family households of cognately related kin were grouped around the house and *marae* of the chief, their senior member. Oliver (1974, 1989) describes such social units, the core of Maohi society, as "kin congregations." The group's lands, as well as its kin-group titles (offices), were identified territorially and symbolically with the kin group's *marae.* Chiefs were vested with stewardship of the land, regulated subsistence activities, redistribution, and public works (roads, bridges, etc.), and negotiated political affairs (warfare, diplomacy, etc.). They also financed groups of skilled craftspeople and other specialists. To support their various activities, they exacted surplus production (and labor) as tribute from commoners.

The households of a particular kin congregation were usually dispersed and separated from each other by gardens and tree crop plantations. In some cases, a number of clustered kin congregations may have formed a loosely constituted village; however, Oliver (1974:44) notes that this was a rare exception and not the rule. In most cases, dispersed households were located along the coastal circumference of islands, or inland along fertile mountain valleys.

Subsistence activities centered on the cultivation of root (taro, sweet potatoes, arrowroot) and tree crops (coconut, breadfruit, bananas, etc.) and on fishing. Women wove pandanus mats and beat bark to make *tapa* cloth; these items were used as household furnishings and clothing. Pigs, chickens, and dogs were the major domesticated animals.

The chief regulated access of group members to the group's corporately owned resources, including land and canoes. For the purposes of communal activities, ritual events, and feasting, the kin congregation pooled its economic efforts under the guidance of its chief. In the course of daily affairs, however, the extended family household was probably relatively independent in garden production and fishing. Although ownership of the land was vested in the group as a whole, individuals and families owned their own cultivated gardens, plantations, taro terraces, and other temporary improvements upon the land; these could be passed on and inherited by their creator's offspring.

In this ambilineal kinship system, an individual's ability to trace a genealogical link through either male or female ties to group founders, as well as coresidence on group territory and effective participation in local affairs, conferred use rights to the kin congregation's lands and other resources. At marriage, young couples could choose to reside with either the bride's or groom's kin, depending on which option offered the greatest economic opportunities (access to land) or political opportunities (affiliation with an important chief). In-marrying spouses possessed all the rights of consanguineal kin in access to resources, including the use of lands, plantations, and other property.

Men and women of the household performed many different tasks, and the sexual division of labor was not rigid (Oliver 1974). Men performed most agricultural labor, went deep-sea fishing, built houses and canoes, engaged in warfare, and cooked food in the earth oven. Women performed light agricultural tasks, wove mats and beat *tapa*, fished in shallow water and on the reef, maintained the household, and cared for children.

▲ Contact, Colonial Incorporation, and Missionary Influence

In the fifteenth century, the newly consolidating European states had started to expand their resource bases and commercial connections around the world and would ultimately impose their political dominion over it. Access to the wealth of Africa, Asia, and the Americas would fill the coffers of these emerging states and fuel the technical and social revolution to be wrought by the imminent Industrial Revolution (see Wolf 1982). European explorers, sailors, and merchants set out to discover new worlds and to beat their competitors to the riches they possessed. Control of the oceans and strategic ports was critical to gaining an advantage in the hostile competition for commercial supremacy.

The renowned wealth of Asia and the Orient had long attracted the Europeans. Following the discovery of the Americas, explorers charted a course around South America and crossed the Pacific. Magellan first traversed it in 1521; other Spaniards followed, eventually occupying the Philippines in 1564.

The Spanish explorer Quiros first sighted the Society Islands in 1606 (Goldman 1970) and, although the islands undoubtedly experienced occasional contacts with European seafarers thereafter, it was not until 1767 that direct, sustained interaction between Maohis and Europeans was established. In that year, the English Captain Wallis, desperate for water and supplies, "committed the ship's boats to sounding out a hostile shore," and spent five weeks on the island of Tahiti. According to Wallis's report, the natives "behaved very insolently, none of them would trust any of our men with any of their things untill they got the nails or toys from them, then several of them would push off and keep all and oythers caried their insolence so high that they struck several of our men" (Newbury 1980:3, citing Robertson 1948:243). Between intermittent commercial transactions, islanders and Wallis's crew traded hostile attacks: "Relations were a volatile blend of cordiality and suspicion, friendship and bloodshed" (Campbell 1989:58; see also Borofsky and Howard 1989:261–262).

The implications of Wallis's visit for Maohi society were immense. Newbury (1980:5) concludes that "in the short space of five days the inhabitants . . . were introduced brutally to the rules of alien commerce, to a totally new level of technology, and to a strange but suggestive indication of permanent settlement. They [islanders] had reacted with hostility but without entirely rejecting what they saw." In particular, islanders coveted the nails (for fishhooks), cloth, ironware, firearms, and liquor that the Europeans offered in exchange for fresh provisions and female companionship.

Wallis was soon followed by the Frenchman Bougainville and then Captain James Cook. Although Cook is well known for his discoveries and extensive exploration of the South Pacific, few know that the major purpose of his early voyages (1769–1777) was astronomical observation (Campbell 1989). Over a span of ten years, he spent a substantial amount of time in the Society Islands, discovered several of the Australs, and explored the Marquesas (Thompson and Adloff 1971). During these visits he (and later visitors as well) introduced European seeds and livestock to islanders, including the Spanish hogs that would become a major trade item with visiting ships (Newbury 1980).

In addition to providing ports of call and provisioning stations, the islands became an important source of specialty trade items coveted by the Chinese, including sandalwood (oil for incense) and trepang (*bêche-de-mer*—sea cucumbers—used as a food and an aphrodisiac). These could be exchanged by the Europeans for the much-sought-after Chinese silks, teas, and spices (Wolf 1982). British whalers had also come on the scene by the 1790s, establishing what would become an important regional South Pacific whaling industry in the first decades of the nineteenth century.

European Interference and Tahitian Political Consolidation

Despite the increasingly heavy volume of trading transactions, direct European influence (and interference) in Maohi society was not felt until 1788, when the *Bounty* mutineers landed on Tahiti, actually took up residence (1789–1791), and traded guns for pork (Goldman 1970:172). Captain Bligh (and later, others) meddled in local political affairs, supporting the ambitions of Tu (Pomare I), a local chieftain bent on military conquest and paramountcy over other chiefs. Through their interference, the Europeans contributed directly to the intensification of civil war and intertribal competition that followed contact. With European support, Tu and his son (Pomare II) would eventually achieve their ambitious goal of Society Islands political unification.

Although intensified warfare was in part responsible for drastically declining population numbers by the end of the eighteenth century, introduced Western diseases had also taken a devastating toll on the Maohi population. On some particularly hard-hit islands, such as the Marquesas, more than 90 percent of the population was lost to recurring epidemics; Oliver (1961:208) notes that of the precontact population of about 80,000, "there were less than 3,000 left [by 1939] to wander around among the ruins." Tahiti and its nearby islands, which conservatively possessed a population of at least 35,000 at contact, could claim only about 10,000 by 1800 (Newbury 1980:32). Early chronicles of this era describe a large number of abandoned *marae* and brush-covered gardens in the interiors of islands, noting that "the remnant of people inhabit[ed] merely the sea-side" (Newbury 1980:32, note 84). The indigenous population would not begin to reestablish itself demographically until well into the twentieth century.

The forces of social transformation escalated dramatically in 1796 with the arrival on Tahiti of the first contingent of pastors from the London Missionary Society. Although islanders generally dismissed their religious teachings, the missionaries went about interfering, as best they could, in the arms trade and in such local customs as human sacrifice and infanticide. Like Bligh, they affiliated themselves with the rising Pomare line of chiefs in hopes of obtaining chiefly patronage, and thus legitimacy, in a society that had tolerated them but was indifferent to their evangelical mission.

Indeed, despite several decades of intense commercial interaction, the Maohi clung closely to their own understandings of the world and of the supernatural, uniformly and consistently rejecting the European's ideology and pretensions of superiority, if not their material goods. While much "commerce in provisions" had taken place, little "commerce in ideas" between the two groups had accompanied it (Newbury 1980:13).

Maohi attitudes are clearly illustrated in one English trader's account of his conversation with Pomare II and his brother, Itia, in 1803 (Turnbull 1813, cited in Newbury 1980). Pomare had pursued the issue of the veracity of the Christian teachings with the trader, demanding to know where Jehovah lived. After receiving his answer, Pomare "said he didn't believe it. His brother was, if possible, still worse. [Itia] was looking on, with a kind of haughty and disdainful indifference. It was all *ha'avare,* or falsehood" (Newbury 1980:13). Newbury (1980:13) goes on to note that in this particular intellectual exchange, "a good deal of Tahitian parochialism [was expressed] for an island which they [the Maohi] declared to be 'the finest part of the whole inhabitable globe.'"

In 1808, Pomare II suffered serious military defeats in his efforts to consolidate the region under his rule and retreated to the island of Moorea. Once there, he "paid greater attention to the teachings of the missionaries, concerned perhaps at the apparent decay of his own *mana* and the loss of the favour of 'Oro [one of the major gods] demonstrated by his own fall" (Campbell 1989:75).

Not long after, in 1812, Pomare officially proclaimed his devotion to

Jehovah (Hanson 1973:7). When he subsequently achieved a major and decisive victory over rival chiefs in 1815 and finally united all of Tahiti, it represented not just a military victory over other chiefs, but a religious victory over their gods as well (Hanson 1973:10). The *mana* of the Christian god was clearly stronger than that of the Maohi gods.

Pomare soon proclaimed Christianity to be the official religion and ordered the destruction of the *marae*. Looking to the missionaries for guidance in the establishment of his new reign, he implemented a "missionary-inspired law code that forbade polygamy, adultery, human sacrifice, and infanticide, and also compelled observance of the Sabbath" (Thompson and Adloff 1971:14). A "politico-religious triumph" of unparalleled magnitude had been wrought: Pomare had achieved political supremacy over the islands, and the foreign missionaries had achieved moral supremacy over the islands' people (Thompson and Adloff 1971:14).

Islanders in the Society Islands, Tuamotus, and Australs converted quickly to Christianity, while only "the cannibalistic Marquesans resisted" (Thompson and Adloff 1971:14). The rapidity of the population's conversion stands in marked contrast to their earlier, persistent disdain for Western religious ideology, and it must be understood within the context of the destablizing events of the previous decades. By 1810, Maohi confidence in their world, like Maohi society itself, had started to crumble. Skepticism about the efficacy of the gods, the very core of the Maohi conceptualization of the world and their place in it, had spread (Newbury 1980). Extensive deaths from introduced disease (against which the Maohi god of healing had proven impotent), depradations resulting from constant civil strife and warfare, and mounting cultural disruptions associated with the European presence had all taken a significant toll on the integrity of island society. Pomare II's military victory in 1815 "under the auspices" of his powerful Christian god dealt the death knell to any remaining confidence in the indigenous gods, opening the way for the acceptance of a new religious order.

The new Christian ideology may have appeared to the Maohi people as a lifeline to salvation in a time of great social stress (see Campbell 1989:73ff), but in truth they had little choice but to accept it. Their own gods had been discredited, and their chiefs, the agents and embodiment of their relationship with the supernatural, had shifted allegiance to the new god.

Although the adoption of the new religion entailed a significant number of social adjustments, most analysts agree that Pomare II intended to retain the basic sociopolitical structure of Maohi society intact. His goal was not to restructure the system, only to install himself at its head (Hanson 1973). And indeed, the new Christian religious system was successfully merged with the indigenous chiefly system. The chiefs, retaining their previous religious role, became the deacons and other leading lay members of the new church. Just as in the precontact era, the established chiefly political hierarchy was sanctioned by religious ideology, although that sanction was now Christian in nature. Thus, the destruction of the traditional gods and the *mana* system did not lead to the disintegration of the chiefly political system (and thus of the basic structure of Maohi society) as many analysts of the early contact era have argued; that process would have to await active French colonial intervention in later decades (Hanson 1973).

Following Pomare II's death in 1821 from alcoholism, he was briefly succeeded by a young son (Pomare III), and then by his daughter (Pomare IV). Pomare IV, who ruled the islands for the next fifty years, was a less capable monarch than her father, and the chiefs were able to expand their powers at her expense. The political centralization achieved by Pomare II began to dissolve.

The French Presence and Protectorate

Pomare IV's inability to rule effectively and to consolidate her kingdom in the mid-1800s was linked to an increasingly prominent European presence in the islands. She found that she was constantly required to negotiate with powerful British and French merchants, ship captains, and political representatives pursuing their own interests in the islands. Even her close affiliation with the British Protestant missionaries did little to protect her from the mounting pressures associated with the steadily more focused European political ambitions in the region.

Although the British had long had a foothold in the islands through the London Missionary Society, the French had come on the scene in greater numbers as their ships came to monopolize a larger share of the trade with South America's western seaboard (Campbell 1989). France also had aspirations of expanding its South Pacific whaling fleet and of enhancing its competitive position in the Asia trade. To achieve these goals, it needed a South Pacific base from which to expand its influence (Newbury 1980).

By the mid-1800s, Europeans' attitudes toward their foreign trading partners and distant sources of supply had shifted. They had come to realize that direct political (and economic) control would be more effective (and lucrative) than the mercantile relationships in place at the time. Thus, an era of European imperialist expansion and empire building in Africa, Asia, and the Pacific ensued (Newbury 1980). The non-Western world was conquered and carved up into European colonies.

In the competition for Pacific colonies and strategic ports, the Marquesas caught France's attention (Newbury 1980). Not only were these northernmost islands ideally situated along major shipping routes but, because their people had successfully resisted conversion by the British Protestant missionaries, they presented an opportunity for the spread of French Catholicism. (Marquesans today are Catholic, while most other Tahitians are Protestant.) In a "calculated act of imperialism" (Campbell

1989:139) common to the era, France annexed the Marquesas outright in 1842.

In the previous decades, the Marquesas had become a center for whalers and blackbirders, and several of its ports were "notorious for their lawlessness and debauchery" (Oliver 1961:209). Island society had been decimated not only by Western diseases, but also by alcohol and the "lawless whites." Thus, a number of Marquesan chiefs were actually pleased to see the French move in, hoping they would bring some order to the islands. Other chiefs, however, fought French control, and only after "many years and many bloody campaigns" did the French finally subdue the islands (Oliver 1961:209).

Anticipating that the British would retaliate for the French annexation of the Marquesas by annexing Tahiti, the French quickly turned their attention there. On Tahiti, French traders and priests had generally been treated as second-class citizens by the Tahitian queen and her British missionary advisers, and they had repeatedly appealed to the French government to protect their interests. In one pivotal incident, British missionaries had a group of French priests ejected from the islands, successfully preventing them from establishing themselves as a rival religious force. The priests, however, returned soon after on a French warship, which "bullied and threatened the Tahitian government" and, "under the threat of the ship's guns they landed and were allowed to stay and to establish their church" (Forman 1988). Less than harmonious relations between the Catholic and Protestant churches have prevailed in the islands to this day.

Queen Pomare IV, protected from French harassment only by the British consul and London Missionary Society missionaries, asked the British government for protection. The British offered sympathy and pledges of moral support, but little more. Seeing an opportunity to move in, the French consul in Tahiti, Moerenhout, and the French warship's admiral, Du Petit-Thouars, "extracted from suborned chiefs and helpless Queen a dictated request for French protection" (Campbell 1989:139; see also de Deckker 1983). The French government acceded to this "request" and declared a protectorate over the islands in 1842. In addition to achieving its goal of securing a major South Pacific base, France believed it had outmaneuvered the British (at least in this instance) in the scramble for Pacific colonies and looked forward to the spread of French Catholicism.

The conditions of the French protectorate called for internal affairs to remain in the hands of the Tahitians and their queen. But the French, long practitioners of a colonial policy of direct rule, did not even so much as maintain a pretense of allowing Tahitians to run their own affairs. When islanders responded with violence to increasing French domination, including a guerrilla war fought by Tahitian warriors in the mountains between 1843 and 1846, the French were given an excuse to intervene directly and to remove uncooperative chiefs. Government-appointed chiefs were contemptuously called *ouioui* (French for "yes yes") by the Tahitians (Danielsson 1983:194). By 1852, the British missionaries had also been removed and replaced by French Protestants.

At about the same time, in 1853, the French declared a protectorate over the large Melanesian island of New Caledonia to the west, which ultimately would become their other major Pacific possession. A strong Catholic mission on the island, as well as French interest in establishing a penal colony there, had motivated the move. There was also growing French nationalist concern over the expansion of British colonial interests in the Pacific and what appeared to be their ambition of turning it into a "British lake" (Campbell 1989:142).

Direct French intervention in Tahitian society and restructuring of its institutions escalated from this date, finally leading to the destruction of the indigenous political system and its replacement by French sociopolitical institutions (Newbury 1980; Hanson 1973). Central to this process was the dismantling of the chiefly aristocracy's power. To this end, the French government abolished tribute payments from the people to the chiefs, dictating instead that the chiefs would be supported by French government stipends. Chiefly succession rules were also discontinued and a system of election (among all chiefs) was instituted. In addition, French courts were introduced that gradually usurped the authority of Tahitian chiefs and judges, even in local Tahitian affairs.

Europeans of this era saw the islands as ideal locations for plantations, and during the decades preceding and during the U.S. Civil War, several cotton plantations were started. In the absence of U.S. competition, cotton became an important regional export for the next several decades. By the 1890s, however, the plantations had declined and were abandoned. Their failure can in part be attributed to Tahitian islanders' disdain for working for wages on plantations and their preference for working on their own lands (see Newbury 1980). To deal with the recurring labor shortages, plantation owners imported Chinese contract laborers to the colony during these years.

Following the demise of the marginal plantation economy, the descendants of the Chinese population moved subsequently into local commerce and import/export businesses. They came to occupy a critical intermediary role between Tahitian commodity producers (of copra, for example) and European businesses (Newbury 1980). On the outer islands, one or two Chinese families typically ran the only existing general stores and monopolized local commerce.

Although the Chinese occupied an important economic niche in the colonial economy, little assimilation among the Chinese, Tahitian, and French populations took place. The Chinese staunchly maintained their own ethnic identity (including religious practices and language), while resentment among Tahitians to the Chinese's growing economic clout grew. In rural areas, Tahitian farmers were commonly in debt to the local Chinese store, typically the only source of canned foods, sugar, and kerosene and the only local buyer of processed copra and other commodities.

In their lack of social assimilation yet occupation of a strategic economic niche, the overseas Chinese in the Tahitian islands were in many ways like a growing number of other Chinese expatriate populations scattered across the Pacific. In the Tahitian islands, as elsewhere, they became a focus of interethnic group conflict and competition. Only in recent decades have ethnic boundaries in French Polynesia relaxed and greater assimilation taken place. By the early 1980s, the Chinese would come to make up about 8 percent of the population of French Polynesia.

Annexation and Assimilation

Finally, "the fiction of an internally autonomous protectorate was dropped" and France annexed Tahiti as a colony in 1881 (Hanson 1973:9). The surrounding islands were annexed as well, including the Leeward group of the Society Islands (in 1888) and the Australs (in 1900 and 1901). Bit by bit, a colony composed of the five main island groups of the region was assembled.

The French pursued a policy of assimilation, incorporating the Tahitian population legally by requiring adherence to the French civil and criminal codes, economically by enforcing a tariff system and other government trade regulations, and culturally by imposing the French language, customs, and educational system (Newbury 1980:204ff). By 1897, the entire system of chiefly titles had been eliminated and island districts were now administered by elected district councils. The head of such councils was the *tavana* (chief), an elected official who functioned as something of a cross between a French mayor and a Tahitian chief. Absolute political power in the new colony, however, was wielded by a French governor who oversaw both internal and external affairs.

Although under the protectorate, land could not be alienated to foreigners, this was soon changed to facilitate economic development. Nevertheless, the resource-poor Tahitian islands, "no Mecca for colonists," attracted few settlers and fewer economic enterprises (Campbell 1989). A small contingent of traders in pearl shell and coconut oil and a few marginal cotton plantations constituted the entirety of the region's commercial development in the first decades following establishment of the protectorate. Except for the islands of Tahiti and Moorea (the centers of foreign influence), land was not alienated to foreigners, but remained under the control of Tahitian families.

The French administration hoped to abolish the kin-based system of joint land ownership still in place in Tahitian communities and to replace it with one of individual ownership. To this end, the French worked to codify the traditional system and to survey parcels. In 1888, land titles were registered for the first time in the names of family heads on a number of islands. Islanders, however, subverted the administration's efforts at individualization by continuing to pass their lands on to their offspring as a group. This process effectively reinstated the system of joint familial ownership.

In their efforts to codify the existing land system, French officials misunderstood the ambilineal system to imply bilateral inheritance (Crocombe 1971a:377–378) and created such a system out of the previous one. Other government-instigated, structural changes took place, but joint, familial ownership based on the traditional system remained entrenched, particularly in rural areas and on outer islands. To Tahitians, the land symbolized fundamental aspects of their worldview and identity, and a strong bond existed between families and their ancestral holdings (see Crocombe 1971a:381).

The traditional land system in rural areas has proven to be quite stable and resistant to change well into the modern era. This can be attributed to a number of factors. In rural areas in particular, the market forces that might have compelled individualization (and land alienation) were absent, as capitalist penetration had been minimal. Islanders continued to make their living much as they had for centuries, and the land system met their needs well. Moreover, land was relatively abundant due to depopulation, so scarcity did not operate as a factor compelling change in the system. Nevertheless, the persistence of a traditionally derived land tenure system greatly at odds with the French view of individual property rights was, and continues to be today, a burr in the side of the administration.

▲ Life in Rural Areas

Although the French had been determined to acquire the territory and implant their own institutions there, they showed little interest in actually governing the far-flung islands (Campbell 1989:165). A succession of indifferent French governors left local affairs mainly in the hands of the missionaries. Working with Tahitian deacons and elected *tavanas,* the missionaries kept community affairs in order. One or more French *gendarmes,* the only resident representatives of a French administration that rarely ventured beyond the environs of Papeete, functioned as official government authorities and shared secular power with the missionaries.

The decrees "that issued from the government offices in Papeete had little impact on [islanders'] lives . . . even if some reached the country districts or outer islands, nobody understood the complicated French jargon. They had no relevance to Polynesian fishermen and planters who, when they needed guidance, sought it in traditional precepts and in the Bible" (Danielsson 1983:195). Although increasingly dependent on Western goods and imports, islanders continued to cultivate their own lands, growing taro and tree crops and fishing much as their ancestors had done for centuries. To acquire cash, they produced and sold small amounts of copra, manioc starch, or fresh foods to local merchants or to passing ships. In the Tuamotus, islanders dived for pearl shell to make money. In the Society Islands, vanilla became an important cash crop for smallholder producers following its introduction in 1848. This pattern of small-scale commodity production by peasant producers has continued to dominate rural island economies to the present day.

Oliver (1961:206) summarizes the economic patterns in place at this time:

> Western capitalists have never been happy about Tahiti. Attempts to set up large plantations have not succeeded: local Polynesians could not be induced to work them, while imported Chinese promptly graduated from wage labor to commerce and eventually came to dominate vegetable growing, merchandising, and service occupations. Most of the copra and vanilla which constituted the colony's major exports was produced by Polynesian householders and sold to Chinese middlemen for overseas marketing, the income being used to buy trade-store calico, kerosene, tobacco, and such things, to supplement the subsistence economy which continued to be the basis for Tahitian native life.

In rural areas, the Christian church was the focus of community social life. In the preceding decades, missionaries from a number of Christian sects, including the Mormons and "Sanitos" (Reorganized Mormons), had arrived and established significant congregations on some islands; the Protestants nevertheless remain the dominant sect on virtually all islands today.

The church was a potent social force in the lives of islanders, dictating social mores, family patterns, and even male-female relations. As Thomas (1987:268) notes, "The transformation of domestic life was certainly on the agendas of both Protestant and Catholic missionaries." At their insistence, the large, precontact extended family was replaced by the more "appropriate" nuclear family. Practices utilized by women to control the numbers and spacing of their offspring, including infanticide and abortion, were prohibited.

Despite the pervasive influence of the missionaries, islanders were not slavish in their formal adherence to Christian ideology. Although devoutly pious and penitent, Tahitians were nevertheless selective in their interactions with the church. Indigenous beliefs in sorcery, ghosts, spirit possession, and other precontact spiritual phenomena, for example, continued. And to the consternation (even today) of pastors, "good" Tahitian Christians consistently declined to participate in church-sanctioned marriages. The traditional pattern that allowed young people to participate in several trial marriages until a compatible partner was found was much preferred.

▲ Into the Twentieth Century

Although we have few documentary sources that describe life in the Tahitian islands at the turn of the twentieth century, Gauguin's colorful paintings allow us to see at least his artist's vision of the islands at that time. Searching for an unspoiled paradise, Gauguin abandoned Europe and took up residence on Tahiti and then in the Marquesas for several years. Vividly depicting the beauty of the islands and what appeared to him to be the simple subsistence activities of Tahitian daily life, Gauguin's canvases do indeed project a kind of paradise that greatly appealed to Westerners.

Yet, Gauguin himself became increasingly disillusioned with what he saw around him. Instead of a true paradise, he came to believe that Tahitian society and culture had been degraded and socially engineered by a pretentious French administration (Newbury 1980:233–234). He was only one among many who, not realizing the extent of postcontact acculturation and cultural transformation, would travel to Tahiti (then and in later years) searching for a Polynesian paradise and finding only disappointment.

A Modern Colonial Economy

By the turn of the century, Papeete had become a vibrant port town that boasted a growing population of French settlers, administrators, and merchants. Centrally located in the expanding entrepôt trade between Sydney, Valparaiso (Chile), and San Francisco, Papeete was the "trading capital of eastern Polynesia" (Newbury 1980:179).

The Tahitian population, however, played little more than a peripheral role in this commercial expansion at the end of the century. The administration was dominated by the French, and trade was largely in the hands of Europeans, although islanders occasionally operated small interisland trading schooners. The European enterprises in the islands, mainly trading ventures and small commerce, required little labor, and so employment opportunities for islanders were rare. A few worked on the Papeete wharves and later (in 1908) in the newly opened Makatea (Tuamotus) phosphate mines. But for the most part, islanders stayed on their own lands, cultivated and fished, and produced export commodities (mainly copra) on a small scale. Thus, unlike the populations of many other Third World regions integrated into the expanding capitalist world economy in the early twentieth century, Tahitians had not been uprooted from their lands or proletarianized (Newbury 1980:235ff).

Despite the active trans-Pacific commerce centered in Papeete, the inherent weaknesses in the colony's economy were becoming readily apparent. It depended entirely on the export of a small number of commodities (copra, vanilla, shell, and phosphates), and these exports were financed by foreign, not local, capital. Moreover, with the exception of phosphates, the colony was only a minor, second-rate producer of its major exports relative to the German, British, and Australian colonies in the Pacific.

The islands had become a part of a dependent, colonial, peripheral economy in which the prices of its exports were determined by levels of consumption and manufacturing in Europe and North America (Newbury 1980:236). As demand and world market prices for the islands' few exports fluctuated, so did the vitality of the fragile regional economy. By the early decades of the twentieth century, the islands had assumed the status of a colonial backwater on the marginal fringes of the world economy.

▲ 3
The Domestication of Tahitian Women

The processes of Westernization set in motion by the European missionaries, colonial officials, and capitalists who came to the islands had a particular and profound impact on Tahitian women's lives. Until recently, it was generally thought that Westernization brought beneficial changes to women, in particular new kinds of economic opportunities, as well as greater social freedom and equality with men. This notion was based in part on the assumption that in non-Western, more traditional societies, women were "servile, dependent, and decidedly inferior to men" (Bossen 1975:587). It was also based on the assumption that women in Western industrial societies play major roles in society and enjoy substantial economic independence and political autonomy.

Work by anthropologists, however, has challenged both of these assumptions. To assess women's relative status in different societies, researchers have sought to isolate a number of key factors that have been found cross-culturally to be associated with high status in society (Etienne and Leacock 1980; Bossen 1975; Sanday 1974). While scholars recognize that social status is multidimensional and influenced by differential participation (and differential valuation of that participation), in a large number of interrelated social spheres (religion, kinship, economic activities, and so on) (Mukhopadhyay and Higgins 1988), a substantial body of cross-cultural data suggests that differential economic participation is one of the most critical factors related to social status.

Research has shown that women tend to have higher status in those societies where their contributions to production (labor, products, etc.) are highly valued and they control strategic resources (through production or distribution of products) (see Sanday 1974; Friedl 1988). In hunting and gathering societies, for example, both men and women produce and control strategic resources, and relations between the sexes are most egalitarian and women possess high social status (Etienne and Leacock 1980).

As society becomes more stratified, control of resources is closely linked not only to high social status but also to political power (authority/ autonomy). Political power is defined here as the ability to shape and direct one's own as well as others' persons and activities, and the ability to participate in major policy decisions (see Schlegel 1977). From a materialist perspective, these factors are closely interrelated; the control of strategic economic resources is the material base from which access to political power and social authority are derived.

It has also been proposed that as societies become more complex, gender relations become more stratified and women become increasingly subordinated to men (Etienne and Leacock 1980). Looking specifically at Western, industrial society, Bossen (1975) has argued that women in modern society actually possess relatively low status (compared to women in more simple societies). She links that low status to male domination of the critical (and powerful) economic and political arenas of society and to women's virtual social isolation in what has become defined as the unimportant household/domestic sphere, the only domain where women are major decisionmakers.

There is a growing body of literature that supports the contention that Westernization is associated with declines in women's social status and their increasing peripheralization in society. In the following analysis of the impact of Westernization on Tahitian women, I isolate the specific mechanisms through which the agents of Westernization—missionaries, colonial officials, and, most important, capitalism—fundamentally altered and redefined women's position in Tahitian society. Not surprisingly, the processes described are not unique to Tahitian society, but reappear consistently in cross-cultural studies of the impact of development and Westernization on women's lives.

▲ Women in Ancient Tahitian Society

Some of the first Europeans to visit the islands—explorers, missionaries, and traders—wrote down their observations of Tahitian society, including their impressions of Tahitian women and how they were treated. In these various chronicles, many of the writers' impressions prove to be mutually contradictory and difficult to sort out. In general, however, they present women as bound by numerous social restrictions and *tapus*, and as inferior to men. The early chroniclers note, for example, that Tahitian men and women ate separately, and while men could eat food prepared by women, women could not eat food prepared by men. Tahitian women were also prohibited from consuming certain choice foods—notably pork and prized fishes and turtles—foods that were frequently offered to the gods and reserved for the aristocracy. At public events women were usually seated behind men and, with the exception of high-ranking women, were excluded from participating in religious activities at the *marae*.

The early sources also noted that female infanticide was common, and that men (and women themselves) sometimes bartered women's sexual favors for European goods. It appeared to the Europeans that Tahitian women were little esteemed by their own society—valued as chattel worth a few nails or a keg of whiskey.

It is important to remember that these early chroniclers saw Tahitian society through their own cultural lenses. In addition to their frequently limited understanding of the Tahitian language and social organization, these writers judged Tahitians (and usually harshly) on the basis of their own relatively puritanical Victorian-era attitudes. Moreover, they ethnocentrically considered islanders to be inferiors and primitives, who would benefit from being "civilized."

Douglas Oliver (1974) has carefully studied and analyzed the early sources, sorting through the numerous details in an effort to distill an accurate and unbiased picture of precontact Tahitian society. He, as well as other scholars who have examined these early sources (Langevin-Duval 1979, 1980, 1990; Thomas 1987; Gunson 1964), agree that far from being oppressed chattel, precontact Tahitian women were socially valued and that they were major actors in social, economic, and political affairs (see also Ortner 1981). In the following analysis, I discuss some of the misconceptions about precontact women, examining the structural and ideological bases of their position in ancient society.

The Ideological Bases of Tahitian Gender Differentiation

In Tahitian religious ideology, the world was divided into the sacred (*ra'a/mo'a*) and the profane/secular (*noa*). Everything associated with spirits (images, *marae,* priests) was *ra'a* or sacred; those things that were not *ra'a* were *noa*. Most important, "*ra'a/mo'a* was dangerous to persons in a state of *noa* and persons in a state of *noa* impaired *ra'a/mo'a*" (Oliver 1974:601). The *arii* were in a perpetual sacred *ra'a* state because of their genealogical closeness to divine ancestors and their great spiritual force, or *mana*. Commoners were normally in a state of *noa*.

Tahitians believed, however, that all men (even those of low rank) could achieve the sacred state (*ra'a*) through ritual, and could therefore associate with the spirits safely. In contrast, women could not achieve the sacred state and were perpetually profane, or *noa*. Because the spiritual world was thus dangerous to women and their presence impaired human interactions with the spiritual world, women were generally excluded from the *marae* and religious activities (except at small family *marae*). High-ranking *ari'i* women, however, were a major exception to this rule; *ari'i* women (like *ari'i* men) were always *ra'a*.

Oliver (1974:601) notes that there is no direct evidence in the primary sources on ancient Tahitian society that might provide the cultural rationale for the Tahitian *ra'a/noa*: male/female distinction. He suggests, however, that women's exclusion from the religious domain may have been related to beliefs common to many Polynesian societies (and more highly elaborated in some Melanesian societies) concerning the dangerous and/or contaminating effects of menstrual blood. Reproductive processes in general were considered to be powerful and dangerous and antithetical to the spiritual world (see Hanson 1982).

In contrast to Oliver's (1974) cautious assessment of the early sources, Langevin's (1990) analysis of them lead her to argue that religious restrictions on women were directly linked to their biological characteristics (see also Shore 1989). She contends that women in ancient Tahitian society were not offered for human sacrifice because their bodies were too impure to present to the gods. Moroever, she concludes that menstrual blood was highly dangerous to males and was disposed of carefully, as was the placenta. Rituals performed at birth were aimed at separating the newborn from dangerous maternal substances and purifying it for entrance into the human world (Langevin 1990:24).

Langevin (1990:25) goes on to propose that feminine contact (*noa*) diminished the effectiveness of masculine pursuits by canceling out the supernaturally derived *mana* that men had sought to bring to those pursuits through ritual. The success of fishing expeditions or warfare, for example, could be placed in jeopardy through contact with the debilitating effects of female *noa*-ness. It is interesting to note, however, that *ari'i* women's divinity/*mana* apparently counteracted, or canceled out, their biologically derived impurity.

In contrast to Langevin's (1990) views on women's contaminating effects and biological "unfitness" for interaction with the supernatural, Hanson (1982) proposes that Polynesian women actually attracted the gods and were "conduits of the sacred." Women specifically "attracted the gods who transformed their generative powers into children" (Hanson 1982). Because of this attraction (as opposed to repulsion), Tahitian women may have been "too close to the gods, too subject to their influence, to be able to control them," and thus women could not "dispassionately manipulate the divine for human ends" as men could (Hanson 1982:375, cited in Howard and Kirkpatrick 1989:83–84). Hanson believes that this interpretation of Tahitian worldview more effectively explains Tahitian women's *noa* status and their exclusion from the *marae*—they needed to be shielded from the supernatural.

We do not know conclusively whether Tahitian society appraised women's biological characteristics positively (as a sacred conduit of the gods and thus dangerous) or negatively (as contaminating and repulsive to the gods and thus dangerous). Nevertheless, it does appear that the social restrictions placed on women were specifically linked to Tahitian society's perceptions of female biology/reproduction—specifically to women's reproductive substances and organs—and not to any notions that women's minds or capacities were inferior (see Langevin 1990:24). Langevin (1990) supports this position by noting that in many Tahitian myths, women figure as prominently and as importantly as men. Tahitian goddesses (like gods) are portrayed as heroes, peacemakers, explorers, inventors of culture, and as personally powerful and adept decisionmakers.

The various eating and food restrictions placed on women were probably also directly related to that aspect of Tahitian worldview surrounding female biological characteristics (and thus to women's *noa* status) (see Shore 1989) and did not indicate a social denigration of women. Oliver (1974:602) suggests that male/female segregation at meals may have been to protect women from the dangers of men's potential sacredness. As Thomas (1987) notes, there is no reason to assume that "either sex imposed [such segregation] on the other . . . nor is it easy to see why this entailed deprivation on the part of women" (Thomas 1987:262). To assume that meal segregation does entail deprivation is to apply Western standards and values to a culturally different case. *Ari'i* women, themselves sacred, could and did eat in the company of men.

Nor should one assume that female infanticide indicated that females were not valued in precontact Tahitian society. Infanticide was typically resorted to when a misalliance between a high-ranking person and an unsuitable person (usually of lower rank) threatened to dilute the *mana*/power of the high-ranking lineage (Langevin 1990). Moreover, anthropologists have long noted that infanticide, as well as other population control mechanisms, is commonly practiced by populous societies whose access to resources is fundamentally circumscribed (as on islands). The choice of females probably reflected the reservation of males for the warfare endemic to many Polynesian chiefdoms.

Moreover, the early writers' conclusion that Tahitian society devalued women because it considered it acceptable for their sexual favors to be sold for a few nails to European sailors reflects a misunderstanding of Tahitian customs and worldview. Tahitians, unlike Victorian-era Europeans, considered sexual freedom to be an important part of young people's lives prior to marriage, and having numerous partners was not unusual (particularly for nonelites). Ortner (1981) suggests that Tahitian women (particularly those of lower rank) would have specifically sought alliances with the Europeans, who were thought to be of superior *mana*. These practices in no way indicated that women were somehow cheaply valued.

Rank and Gender

Although Tahitian society probably believed that women's biological processes made them unsuited (or unsafe) for interaction with spirits and deities, this belief—and the gender-based differentiation that resulted—did not carry over negatively into the critical structural principles that determined an individual's social status or rank. This suggests that women's supposed contaminating effects were relevant in only a limited number of social arenas, mainly those connected to food and to the spiritual world. The *ra'a/noa* distinction had no bearing on one's ascribed social position/power (rank) in precontact Tahitian society.

Indeed, the early chroniclers describe the great social prestige and political power wielded by some high-ranking women—occasionally "laws unto themselves" (Oliver 1974:605). Women could achieve sociopolitical prominence because the genealogical principles that determined one's rank in society were applied in a similar way to both males and females. First-born offspring, male or female, inherited the greatest quantity of *mana* from their parents and thus were higher ranking than later-born offspring. Moreover, in the claims of various kin lines to high chiefly titles, female links were just as valued and important as male links.

Although in principle both high-ranking males and females could inherit chiefly titles, males usually held these positions. One of the chief's most critical duties was to communicate with life-giving spirits and deities, an activity considered most appropriate to men. Men also dominated political affairs, a pattern that may have been associated with chronic warfare. Typically, *ari'i* women achieved prominence and authority as sages, genealogists, and curers; but in a few cases, they did lead warriors into battle (Oliver 1974). Because rank was more important than gender in determining differential power and social prerogatives, high-ranking women dominated both men and women of lower rank.

Kin Congregations and Relations of Production

Within the domain of the large cognate kin group (kin congregation) and extended family households, male/female relations appear to have been characterized by a pattern of male authority (Oliver 1974:604) accompanied by significant personal autonomy for women. Male authority at both the kin-group (chiefdom) and household levels appears to have been related to their supervision of productive activities and to their role as mediator with the life-giving supernatural. It does not appear, however, that male domestic authority extended to direct control over persons, particularly adults of equal rank. Women, for example, possessed significant individual rights and freedoms, including the ability to make independent decisions concerning marriage, divorce, abortion, infanticide, and sexual relationships (Oliver 1974; Thomas 1987; Langevin-Duval 1979, 1980; Gunson 1964).

In the organization of work and control of the products produced by the domestic group, it appears that male/female relations were characterized by cooperation and sharing. Although productive tasks were differentiated by sex, both men and women were active in all spheres of production and sometimes performed each other's tasks (except canoe fishing).

As noted in the previous chapter, men performed most agricultural work, went fishing, built houses and canoes, and cooked food in the earth oven. Women performed occasional and light agricultural tasks, wove mats and beat *tapa,* gathered shellfish on the reef, prepared foods to be cooked by men, maintained the household, and cared for children. In general, "the Maohis appear to have been pragmatists with regard to most of their productive activities, adjusting their work contributions to the physical capabilities [i.e., requirements] of the work rather than to any arbitrary and inflexible notions of what individuals should do in terms of their sex" (Oliver 1974:602).

Most important, it appears that female contributions to the domestic economy were as highly valued as those of men. As the division of labor suggests, males and females made separate, yet complementary, contributions of objects and services to the joint household economy. Ultimately, all contributions were pooled and shared, and Oliver (1974:602) concludes that the transactions between males and females of the same domestic unit appear to have been characterized by "mutuality rather than exploitation."

In general, there is no evidence to suggest that either sex dominated control of the means of production. Indeed, Oliver (1974) suggests that the domestic economy was one in which both men and women were the relatively independent producers and owners of both consumables (mainly food) and durable goods (tools, barkcloth, mats, etc.). Men and women controlled some resources independently. The most notable example of this was breadfruit trees. Tools and other capital items used by individuals were probably the property of the person who made them. In a culturally similar case, Linnekin (1986:3) describes the precontact Hawaiian woman as a "member of a community of owners of the means of production: an equal, an adult among adults, a decision-maker."

In ancient Tahitian society, there would have been little rationale for individual members of households to accumulate wealth (at the expense of other household members) or to dominate the means of production. The activities of the household were geared toward fulfilling subsistence needs and producing a surplus to be given as tribute to chiefs. All individuals, male and female, had rights to land and other resources by virtue of their kinship ties. But most important, social rank was ascribed at birth and could not be altered through wealth accumulation or other means.

The Status of Women in Precontact Society

While it is possible to identify a pattern of male preeminence in particular social spheres, notably politics and religion, it does not appear reasonable to infer from it that females were socially subordinated to males or devalued by Tahitian society. Moreover, women apparently were important actors and decisionmakers in numerous social spheres; high-ranking women in particular made their presence felt throughout precontact society. Oliver (1974:604) concludes: "A careful reading of the sources leaves me with the impression that many Maohi [indigenous Tahitian] women were in actuality ('historically,' in Western terms) anything but a passive, deferential, submissive lot: certainly not in domestic matters and often not in 'public' affairs either."

Perhaps most important, there appears to have been no gender-based differentiation in control of the means of production (e.g., men but not women owned land) or in the valuation of male versus female contributions to the domestic economy. Thus, there is no evidence to suggest that women were economically dependent on men, a key factor related to patterns of male domination in many societies.

Rampant inequalities based on differential control of the means of production (land, canoes, plantations, etc.) did pervade ancient Tahitian society, but they were based on differences of rank, not gender. As noted above, high-ranking women enjoyed all of the social, economic, and political prerogatives of high-ranking men. Some of them also enjoyed the same degree of sociopolitical power in ancient chiefdoms.

▲ Women in Neo-Tahitian Peasant Society

During the colonial era, fundamental changes took place in Tahitian society that would cause women's relatively high status to deteriorate and would cause women to be increasingly moved out of important social arenas and relegated to a devalued domestic sphere.[1] Some of the changes were implemented by the missionaries who sought to eradicate what they considered to be heathen practices and to replace them with a moral and Christian domestic life. Other changes came about as French colonial officials worked to replace indigenous sociopolitical institutions with French institutions. And some of the most critical changes in women's roles and status took place as Tahitian communities were integrated into the regional and world market systems. Islanders began producing commodities and working for wages in the expanding capitalist economy Europeans had transplanted to the islands.

Missionaries and Domestic Life

The missionaries made much of what they took to be Tahitian women's oppression in precontact society and advanced the notion that their situation would greatly improve following conversion (Thomas 1987). As Christians,

Tahitian women would no longer be degraded through their practice of pagan and amoral customs (infanticide, etc.), and they would be released from arbitrary *tapus* and religious restrictions. Moreover, they would become full-fledged members of the church.

The early chroniclers noted that Tahitian women did indeed flock to church in large numbers, greatly outnumbering men in the early congregations (Thomas 1987). But although women may have been *in* church, they were not allowed to play any meaningful role in its organization or direction. Following the European pattern, church officials deemed that women were not suited to be pastors, deacons, or other lay church leaders, and men held these positions.

It is also difficult to see how other changes implemented by the missionaries improved women's situation. This is particularly true of imposed changes in the organization of domestic life. The prohibition on infanticide and abortion caused women to lose some of the control they had had over the numbers and spacing of their children. The missionary-inspired shift from the extended to the nuclear family meant that women became individually responsible for all childcare and household maintenance and were no longer able to share that responsibility with other women of the household. And in general, the missionaries proselytized their own Victorian-era attitudes of female submissiveness and sub-ordination to the male head of the family. Consequently, the personal freedoms women had once enjoyed concerning decisions about marriage, divorce, and sexual relationships disappeared; these matters became subject to the authority of husbands and fathers and to the authority of the church.

The missionaries also encouraged major changes in the productive activities of men and women. Believing that cultivation was "unsuitable to [the female] sex" and that women's other economic activities were "derogatory to the female and inimical to an improvement in morals," the missionaries decided that "men should dig, plant, and prepare the food, and the women make cloth, bonnets, and attend to the householdwork" (Ellis 1831, III:392–393, cited in Thomas 1987). Work "in the household" became defined as that appropriate to women—particularly household maintenance and childcare.

To keep women busy at their "appropriate" tasks, missionaries' wives organized new activities for them (Langevin 1990:34). Tahitian women were taught to sew dresses (to be worn to church), a more decent garment in the eyes of the missionaries than the Tahitian *pareu* (length of cloth wrapped around the waist). Missionaries' wives also taught Tahitian women to sew quilts (*tifaifai*) and to fabricate European-style ladies' hats (also to be worn to church) using their traditional weaving (pandanus) techniques. And women were encouraged to attend Bible school where they could learn to read and write the Scriptures.

Colonialism and Structural Change

In Neo-Tahitian peasant communities, new positions of community leadership emerged as the Christian church became socially powerful and as French officials dismantled the chiefly system. In most Tahitian communities, missionaries and lay pastors shared power with elected mayors (*tavanas*), village councils, and local police (*mutoi*). But as in the case of the church, colonial administrators did not consider women to be suitable (or capable) public representatives. Thus, only Tahitian men held these positions and women were effectively excluded from political positions of community leadership.

In addition to political changes, French restructuring of the indigenous land tenure system effectively created a system of bilateral inheritance (as noted in the previous chapter). Offspring, male and female, would inherit land from both their parents.

Land inheritance may be the only example of where French efforts to refashion Tahitian society actually preserved the essence of the ancient system—the principle that both males and females were equally valid in the transmission of rights to property/resources from one generation to the next. In Neo-Tahitian peasant society, both men and women were considered to be owners of land.

In addition, residence continued to be flexible; young couples could choose at marriage to reside on the familial lands of either the bride or groom. The choice was usually determined by who had the most land, and uxorilocal residence was just as common as virilocal residence. An in-marrying husband or wife possessed full rights to use the familial land and other resources of his or her spouse.

▲ Market Integration and Commodity Production

In the island communities that now made up the French colony, available market-oriented economic opportunities varied greatly, depending on natural resources and distances to Papeete markets. In the Tuamotu atolls, islanders earned money by processing copra and diving for shell (Danielsson 1955), while in the Society Islands they sold vanilla, pandanus roof thatchplates, and fish (Oliver 1981; Finney 1973). In the case of the Society Islands, particularly those near Tahiti, some wage work was also available. In the distant Australs, islanders sold coffee and fresh foods to passing schooners (Marshall 1961). For the most part, the newly created Tahitian peasantry pursued any activity that would bring in the money needed to purchase much-coveted Western manufactured items, imported foods, and luxury items (liquor, tobacco, etc.).

In Tahitian peasant communities, the independent and usually nuclear family household was the unit of production and consumption, mixing its commodity production or wage labor with subsistence-oriented agriculture and fishing. The latter continued to fulfill most of the peasant family's subsistence needs.

Households and Changing Relations of Production

The adoption of new kinds of cash-earning activities, the reorientation of productive efforts from fulfilling subsistence needs (and supplying the tribute due to chiefs) to producing a marketable surplus, and the new importance of money brought about fundamental changes in men's and women's productive roles. Despite missionaries' admonitions that men should dig and plant and women should do the "householdwork," both men and women worked in the production of many kinds of market commodities. Both worked in the vanilla fields, dove for shell, gathered coffee, and worked in making pandanus roof thatchplates (to be sold for newly constructed housing and hotel bungalows). On the other hand, only men worked in the processing of copra and in commercial fishing. The vast majority of all wage jobs (usually on plantations) were held by men, although women were occasionally hired as domestics by Europeans.

In addition to commodity production, men continued to perform most agricultural labor in subsistence-oriented taro gardens, and also fished for family consumption. Women were responsible for childcare and the maintenance of the household (cleaning, manufacturing mats and other household items, sewing and washing clothes, preparing food); they also performed secondary tasks in subsistence gardens and occasionally fished on the reef.

Men dominated most cash-earning activities and controlled most cash income, despite women's substantial contributions to both subsistence and commodity production (see Lockwood 1988a). Women's work had been redefined as being "in the household"—even though they were frequently in the gardens, on the reef, or in the tree crop plantations.

In the case of vanilla cultivation, men planted and cared for vanilla gardens, while women frequently specialized in the "tiring and boring" job of blossom-by-blossom pollination (Oliver 1981:131). Despite the fact that both men and women worked in the gardens, men were defined as the owners of the gardens, because according to Tahitian principles, gardens were owned by the individual who created (planted) them. This was true regardless of who owned the land on which they were planted. In cases where a wife might actually own the land where her husband's vanilla gardens were located, the husband, as "owner" of the vanilla, would take the vanilla to market and control the money that was earned. In some cases, men would give their wives a small portion of the harvest to sell for themselves (see Lockwood 1988a).

Male control of copra income was more problematic because both men and women inherited ownership rights (again, jointly with other kin) in coconut plantations from parents and grandparents. Thus, a wife, not her husband, might be the owner of the plantation where her husband made copra. This was particularly likely if the couple resided on her familial lands. But men performed all phases of copra processing and women were virtually excluded from production; islanders said that the work was too hard for them (but women process copra in other Pacific island societies). Men were thus able to control copra earnings because they could claim that it was their labor alone that had produced the copra.

In the fabrication of pandanus roof thatchplates, women prepared and processed the pandanus that men would then weave into thatchplates and sell, keeping the money. Weaving had traditionally been a female activity, but men began to participate when a market for the thatchplates developed.

When opportunities to sell fish were available, men also controlled this source of income, since only men ventured out in the outrigger canoes. And most wage jobs went to men (mostly on plantations) because the Europeans believed that the work was too difficult for women and that they belonged at home caring for the household and children.

Male domination of market-oriented production and cash income also meant that they purchased and were considered the owners of major capital tools and equipment (see Oliver 1981). Although capital investment in commodity production was not extensive, some men did buy copra dryers, small trucks, motorboats, and building materials. Thus, men were defined as the owners of these means of production.

Cash Income and Household Authority

In the Tahitian peasant household, male control of familial cash income was (and is) the foundation upon which men's differential authority and decisionmaking rights as heads of the household rested. Women and children were financially dependent and thus subordinate to husbands and fathers.

The relationship between control of income and authority can be clearly seen in the ethnographic sources on Tahitian peasant society, and Finney (1973) has described it for the case of 'A'ou'a. In 'A'ou'a, a community located near the major road into Papeete, many men and some women had obtained wage jobs. Finney explains the situation in which both husband and wife were employed: "Such a division of income earning is often accompanied by a weakening of the husband's authority, and, in a few extreme cases where the wife has become the main provider in the family [i.e., the husband earned less money or did not have a job], by women of the household assuming major authority" (Finney 1973:83). He goes on to say, "This gain in authority is resisted by some men, and disagreements over family authority between a working man and his wife appear to be the cause of many recent family quarrels" (1973:84). One of Finney's Tahitian women informants summed it up: "Money gives authority" (1973:84).

The relationship between income control and authority in the Neo-Tahitian household was (and is) strong. This was probably due to the general importance of money and consumer goods, as well as to the weakness of other noneconomic bases of authority. In the precontact family, male preeminence had been supported by their managerial role in production and by indigenous religious principles. In the peasant community, male preeminence was supported only by Christian ideological precepts that proclaim that a man is head of his family. Tahitian women nevertheless strove to have a say in household and public affairs when this was possible.

Women gained some political leverage in the household domain through their ownership of land and their husbands' dependence on their labor contributions in commodity production. Regarding land, Oliver (1981:322) notes that some women "exercised much initiative in family cash-income enterprises, sometimes in spite of and sometimes in accord with their husbands' wishes. This last situation most frequently prevailed in families where women owned most of the land."

The examples of male/female relations in the peasant household described by Oliver (1981) suggest that once men met their responsibility for fulfilling the family's subsistence needs, they then used any remaining cash income as they wished. Women may or may not have been consulted about expenditures. Many Tahitian women sought their own independent sources of cash income, which they could expend according to their own priorities. Those activities, however, were necessarily small-scale pursuits like selling eggs or pandanus mats.

Men and women typically kept their incomes separate, and it appears that once household subsistence needs were met, men and women had quite different consumption priorities. Men purchased liquor, radios, and cigarettes, while women bought dresses, sewing materials, and items for their children (see Oliver 1981). Similar patterns have been documented in other developing communities (see Charlton 1984; Nash 1977; Schuster 1982). In general, male income is frequently not used to raise familial subsistence levels (i.e., quality of food, clothing, etc.) as is women's income in many cases, but is instead expended on luxury consumer items, such as radios, motorbikes, and so on.

Male domination of cash-earning activities and income was probably facilitated by other changes, which meant that women were increasingly tied to the household. Ember (1983) has argued, for example, that women's domestic tasks proliferate as families in developing communities begin accumulating Western manufactured goods. Maintaining the household becomes a more time-consuming task. And changes in reproductive practices (prohibitions on abortion, etc.) may have also meant that women experienced more pregnancies, bore more children, and had less control over birth spacing.

The New Ideology of Male Provider/ Female Maintainer of the Household

The Western ideology of male provider/female maintainer of the household had become well entrenched in Tahitian peasant society by the first half of the twentieth century (see Thomas 1987). This was true despite women's various productive contributions to "provisioning" the family. As a statement of appropriate domestic life, this artificial dichotomy was promoted by Christian missionary teachings. But it also reflected a new conceptual distinction between a male-dominated, formal productive sphere and a female-centered, domestic/reproductive sphere in Tahitian peasant society.

There is also evidence to suggest that women's labor in the newly designated domestic sphere was devalued relative to men's labor in the "productive" sphere. Based on a comparison of male and female contributions to the Tahitian peasant household economy, Oliver (1981:329–330) concludes:

> The principle that clearly emerges from this comparison is that a man's services, time for time, received a higher valuation than his wife's in the transaction formula of domestic pool-sharing. A woman had to work longer than her husband to fulfill her obligations and judging by my rough measure this time was about three to two.

Where women contributed some money to the household economy, Oliver (1981:330) says:

> Yet despite the fact that a *tara* (five francs) earned by a woman would buy as much bread or tinned meat as the one earned by her husband, it was not usually evaluated as highly as the latter, i.e., it did not reduce the woman's other domestic obligations to the extent that it reduced those of her husband. A man working steadily for wages was excused from carrying out many other domestic tasks ordinarily carried out by men, whereas a woman income earner simply had to work longer.

The picture that emerges is a familiar one; women's productive activities in the household were not "work."

▲ Westernization, Capitalism, and Women

The patterns that have been described are not unique to rural Tahitian society, but recur repeatedly in non-Western societies in the process of Westernization. Essentially, Westernization (synonymous with "modernization") involves the adoption of Western institutions and values by culturally different, non-Western peoples. In addition to Western technology and material goods, the package typically includes Western social and political institutions, as well as capitalism and the concept of private property. During the colonial era, Westernization also usually involved the conversion to Christianity.

From a materialist perspective, the key processes in women's relative subordination with Westernization are the changes in productive/economic relations that accompany integration into capitalist markets—in other words, the changes that accompany the penetration of capitalist relations of production (see Fernandez-Kelly 1981; Caulfield 1981; Afonja 1981; Bossen 1984; Reiter 1975). The other social, political, and religious/ideological changes that also take place during Westernization—changes in secondary institutions—reinforce and justify the fundamental changes that have taken place in the core economic/subsistence sphere.

Replication of Capitalist Relations of Production in the Household

In a capitalist system, a relatively small elite owns the means of production (land, etc., all of which is private property), separating most people from direct access to or control over the resources they require to fulfill their subsistence needs. Lacking access, the latter group sell the only resource they do control—their labor—to the owners of the means of production (capitalists); in exchange they receive their subsistence, usually in the form of wages. In this system, the goods produced by labor are defined as belonging not to the laborer, but to the owners of the means of production. Because they control resources and material wealth in this stratified system, the capitalist class are economically and politically powerful in society; they effectively usurp the authority to make public policy and control community affairs. In contrast, the laboring class, the proletariat, are not only relatively impoverished, socially subordinate, and economically dependent, but they are politically powerless.

As non-Western societies become integrated into market systems, these capitalist relations of production are replicated at the local community level, replacing indigenous economic systems. They also become replicated within the basic unit of production and consumption, the peasant household.

Capitalist relations of production can be replicated within the commodity-producing peasant household because that household embodies both the functions of capital (it owns its own means of production: land, tools, etc.) and of labor (production). Inherent in the household unit, then, is the potential for internal stratification based on the differential assumption of the role of capitalist by certain members of the household and the role of labor by others.

Indeed, the pattern that has been documented in many developing areas, including rural Tahitian society, is that males come to dominate new kinds of market-oriented production, are defined as the owners of strategic resources, and control the products of household labor, particularly cash income (Boserup 1970; Nash 1977; Fernandez-Kelly 1981; Charleton 1984). Thus, they have essentially taken on the role of capitalist. This is true regardless of women's labor contributions to market production. Women essentially perform the role of labor, exchanging their labor in production and reproduction for their subsistence (food, clothing, and other necessities furnished by the male head of the household).

In addition, women's labor in reproduction and domestic activities is devalued (and unremunerated) because in capitalist systems, the "concept of labor [is] reserved for activity that produces surplus value[2] (i.e., cash-earning activities) (Mies 1982:2). Men dominate a formal and public "productive" sphere (where money is earned, profits are made, and capital accumulated), and women are increasingly relegated to a devalued domestic sphere where no "work" takes place. As Sacks (1974:211) notes, women's "labor [is] a necessary but socially subordinate part of producing an exchangeable surplus."

Moreover, as in all capitalist systems, differential power (decision-making ability, authority) in the household is critically linked to control of the means and rewards of production. Male control of resources, and

A Tubuai woman and her small grandson watch canoe races (photo: Lance Rasbridge).

especially of cash income, makes women and children their economic dependents and thus political subordinates. The household becomes characterized by a patriarchal pattern of male authority and decisionmaking prerogatives.

In Tahitian communities, this pattern was consistent with and reinforced by patriarchal Christian ideology, which dictated that men were heads of families, with women and children rightfully subordinate to them, and that women's domain was the domestic sphere. Female subordination was also reinforced by women's exclusion from leadership roles in the community and church and from many wage jobs. This exclusion mirrored practices characteristic of patriarchal European society at the time.

▲ Notes

1. Other sources that describe the negative impact of colonialism on Pacific island women are Gailey 1987 and Jolly and MacIntyre 1989.

2. Surplus value is defined (following Roseberry 1976:50) as the difference between the value of the product of labor (usually measured as market value) and the value of the labor power that produced the product. Capitalists retain the surplus value, while labor receives only wages, the market value of its labor. Women's domestic/reproductive labor creates no marketable product and thus no surplus value in a capitalist system.

▲ 4
French Agendas: Nuclear Colony and Welfare State Colonialism

The patterns of Tahitian gender stratification, familial relationships, and peasant community organization that evolved following Western contact changed little during the last part of the nineteenth and first half of the twentieth centuries. This era of relative social stability was generated by isolation—an isolation that reflected the region's highly marginal position on the fringes of the world economy. Rural Tahitian men's and women's lives revolved around provisioning their families and earning money from small-scale commodity production, and around active participation in the Christian church.

But starting in the 1960s, this isolation ended abruptly as France embarked upon its comprehensive plan to develop and modernize the islands and to restructure its political relationship with them. This unprecedented surge of direct French neocolonial intervention in Tahitian society was promoted in part by France's increasingly problematic status as one of the last remaining colonial powers in the world. It was also directly linked to the French state's evolving agendas in the international political and nuclear arenas.

▲ The "Modernization" of French Colonialism

Following World War II, the growing movement for worldwide decolonization gathered momentum, and France came under increasing pressure to release its foreign possessions. Not wishing to do so, yet hoping to curtail criticism, France liberalized its policies toward its possessions. French Polynesia was officially designated as a territory of France, and its people were granted a representative assembly and French citizenship. Nevertheless, emerging Tahitian nationalism and steady deterioration of the territory's economy following the war generated the region's first and only independence movement in the 1950s (see Thompson and Adloff 1971).

That movement was doomed to failure, however. In the years since the war, France had been pumping more and more money into the economically stagnant territory until it was virtually supporting it financially (paying for government services and so on), and its dependency was absolute. When President de Gaulle agreed to a referendum vote on independence in all of France's overseas dependencies, the Tahitian population voted for continuing political affiliation with France. They feared the loss of French financial support that political independence would bring.

The territory was then literally catapulted into the modern era when, in the early 1960s, France decided to build its nuclear testing installation, Centre d'Expérimentation du Pacifique (CEP), in the Tuamotu islands. One could readily argue that the consequences of the CEP for Tahitian society have been only slightly less momentous than the unexpected arrival of the Europeans several centuries earlier. The CEP would generate an unprecedented era of economic growth and associated social change. France simultaneously implemented "welfare state colonialism" (see Bertram and Watters 1985)—a new form of neocolonial dependency relationship—in its "nuclear colony."

The Postwar Evolution of the Economy

In the years after World War II, the territory's economic situation had deteriorated. Overseas competition and the invention of synthetic substitutes had led to falling prices for copra and other territorial exports. As 80 percent of the territory's income depended on customs duties levied on its exports, government revenues had shrunk. The Makatea phosphate mines, although a major exporter of phosphates, were contributing little to the general economy because the bulk of their profits were repatriated to Europe and its owners hired mostly foreign labor (Thompson and Adloff 1971); the mines would be largely exhausted by the 1960s anyway.

The Papeete port had expanded in shipping and commercial activities, exposing serious deficiencies in its infrastructure, including roads, communication networks, and support systems like hospitals and schools. Moreover, in the postwar years, influxes of outer islanders searching for wage work and other opportunities had begun to crowd Papeete. The growing rural exodus had also contributed to a pattern of steadily declining productivity in the agricultural sector and had promoted a growing dependence on imported foods. Lacking a developed manufacturing/industrial sector, the territory was already heavily dependent on imports of manufactured goods as well as petroleum products.

After the war, France had begun a serious program for the economic development of its overseas dependencies, but its impact was not felt in French Polynesia until the late 1950s (see Thompson and Adloff 1971). Not surprisingly, French concern for the well-being and development of its territorial population coincided with the short-lived Tahitian independence movement of the 1950s.

Government planners realized that in addition to much-needed modernization of the territory's infrastructure, serious measures would have to be taken to develop the stagnant economy and curtail skyrocketing levels of importation, to reduce rural out-migration and urban crowding, and to generate employment opportunities (in agriculture, light industry, and tourism) for the growing population. Planners also realized that the territory did not have the resources required to effect its own "modernization," and that France would have to finance it. By 1959, "there were no further illusions as to the country's ability to finance any appreciable part of its own development program. The funds from France [previously loans] became outright subsidies" (Thompson and Adloff 1971:83). A series of five-year plans was formulated to implement economic growth and development in the region (e.g., Service du Plan 1975).

▲ Nuclear Colony

At the close of World War II, France vowed never again to be dependent on its allies for protection, and it determinedly pursued the creation of its own independent nuclear strike force capability (Tagupa 1976). Following the independence of the former French colony of Algeria and France's loss of its desert testing installations there, a new location was sought, and the remote Tuamotu atolls of French Polynesia appeared ideal.

The territory's urgent need for infusions of capital to promote development, its small and remote population, and its well-established political and economic dependency on France were factors that undoubtedly contributed to President de Gaulle's decision to build the CEP in the region. It was to a group of French Polynesian delegates seeking more financial aid for the territory that de Gaulle announced his decision in the early 1960s.

Although the Tahitian population voiced opposition to having a nuclear installation in its midst, this was soon defused by the increasing aid packets and economic boom that accompanied the CEP's construction. In order "to make the CEP more acceptable to the islanders, the General agreed not only to meet the budgetary deficit and take over the cost of the territory's secondary schools and communication services, but also to finance the expanded public works programs" (Thompson and Adloff 1971:84).

A massive investment of French capital and technology was required for the building of the CEP and its extensive support facilities, which included several military bases. Ultimately, the CEP would be responsible for bringing a new international airport, an expanded port, a major regional hospital, and modern transportation and communication networks to the territory. Thousands of high-paying jobs were created for islanders seeking wage employment. The 1960s were a decade of unparalleled growth and prosperity throughout the territory.

The new employment opportunities generated by the CEP led many islanders to abandon their traditional Tahitian lifestyle of taro farming and fishing and to adopt one based on urban wage employment. Levels of production (agriculture and commodity exports) fell to all-time lows; this trend would continue to the present. Between the early 1960s and the end of the decade, copra exports fell from 25,000 metric tons to 16,000 tons; coffee exports from 114 tons to none (in 1965); shell exports from 645 tons to 185 tons; and vanilla exports from 180 tons to 28 tons (Blanchet 1984). At the same time, imports increased dramatically. Whereas in 1961 exports covered 70 percent of the cost of imports, by the early 1970s this ratio had declined to about 10 percent (Henningham 1989a:108). The mounting trade deficit had become a considerable burden on the already fragile regional economy.

The CEP also promoted the development of other distortions in the regional economy, problems that have remained largely unresolved to the present. The unprecedented demand for labor and the high wages paid for it generated massive rural out-migration (Connell 1985:21); this directly contributed to rural economic stagnation. Between 1956 and 1967 alone, the population of Papeete almost doubled, growing from about 23,000 to over 44,000 residents. Most of this increase was the result of in-migration from rural areas and outer islands (Connell 1985:36). (Over 70 percent of the territory's population, approximately 120,000 people, now lives on Tahiti [Henningham 1989a:108]).

Moreover, the CEP promoted rampant inflation and a rapidly escalating cost of living throughout the territory. Between 1959 and 1965, the overall cost of living in Papeete had risen 39 percent; the cost of local foodstuffs had risen by 80 percent and rents by 60 percent, and the price of urban land had doubled (Thompson and Adloff 1971:137–138).

Rural migrants seeking employment in Papeete, most of whom possessed little formal education and few job-related skills, suffered most acutely from the rising cost of living. Because migrants owned no land, they were forced to pay high land and house rents and were unable to supplement their incomes through subsistence agriculture and fishing. The city's outskirts were transformed into slumlike shantytowns, where migrants lived in deplorable conditions (Tagupa 1976:203). Social isolation, unstable employment, and urban poverty encouraged the proliferation of crime, delinquency, and other social problems (see Ringon 1971).

Urban poverty and rising unemployment have continued to be major social problems in the territory. Striking dockworkers and gangs of unemployed youth took part in a riot in 1987 that left the Papeete business area looking like a war zone. Earlier, in 1983, there were disturbances arising from a strike by hotel employees. Strikers' mounting anger was fueled by poverty and disillusionment (Henningham 1989a:108; see also Crocombe and Hereniko 1985).

▲ **Regional Development
Planning and Economic Growth**

Development planning from the 1960s to the present has reflected growing concern over the territory's long-standing economic problems, as well as over the significant socioeconomic dislocations caused by the CEP. The territory's five-year development plans outlined growth in tourism, light industry, and agriculture (e.g., Service du Plan 1970, 1975). In the 1960s and 1970s, several small industries geared largely toward import substitution were developed on Tahiti, including a coconut oil processing plant, a brewery, and an orange juice plant. Nevertheless, intractable problems linked to small population size, distances to markets, transport inefficiencies, lack of access to raw materials, and deficiencies in hydroelectric power have plagued, and will continue to plague, the problematic growth of industry in the territory (see Connell 1985).

One important exception to this has been the growth of the commercial gathering of shell and black pearls in the Tuamotu atolls. Although largely run by Asian firms, exports of black pearls were second only to exports of copra in the 1970s, and in 1981 their export earnings (405 million CFP—French Polynesian or Pacific francs) equaled those of copra oil exports (Connell 1985:5). Copra production itself has steadily fallen, stabilizing at about 16,000 metric tons exported in 1981.

Although planners have consistently looked to tourism as an area for potentially rich development, it too has been fraught with fluctuating and problematic patterns of growth (see Blanchet 1984:82). The construction of the international airport at Faaa (Papeete) in the early 1960s and foreign investment in luxury hotels facilitated a rapid initial expansion in the industry. Before 1960, one could reach Tahiti only by taking a propeller aircraft to the island of Bora Bora (landing on the World War II airstrip there) and then transferring to a seaplane for the short flight to Tahiti. At that time, tourists could find lodging only in a small number of bungalow-type, family-run hotels; in the 1970s and 1980s, high-rise, luxury hotel towers would replace them.

Whereas in 1960 Tahiti received only 4,000 tourists, by 1982 that number had risen to 114,000 (Connell 1985). It was expected that the total number of hotel rooms would increase from about 2,000 in 1985 to 4,000 in 1989, although plans had anticipated an ever-greater growth. Indeed, planners' optimistic projections for expansion in the tourist industry have consistently failed to materialize. While numbers of hotel rooms have been on the increase, numbers of tourists have been on the decline in recent years. Between 1986 and 1987, tourist arrivals fell by 11 percent, and were expected to fall (but less dramatically) in 1988 to about 140,000 (*Europa World Yearbook* 1989). The remoteness of the region, as well as its well-earned reputation for being expensive relative to more accessible and less import-dependent tropical islands, has discouraged tourism.

Although it is estimated that the tourist industry's contribution to the economy is three times the value of territorial exports (*Europa World Yearbook* 1989), its actual contribution to regional development has been questioned. Most hotels are owned by foreign multinational firms and are thus financed and run by external interests. While tourism has created employment opportunities, Tahitians participate in this industry mainly in the capacity of menial or unskilled service personnel (see Robineau 1977) and receive few of the economic benefits it generates. Moreover, there has been growing concern throughout the region, as well as in many other Pacific island nations, about the cultural degradation that frequently accompanies the development of tourism (see Finney and Watson 1975).

In addition to the hoped-for growth of industry and tourism, planners sought to shift what remained of the flagging agricultural sector from its previous export orientation (copra, vanilla, etc.) to production for the expanding regional market. Urban population growth, as well as the arrival of CEP personnel and tourists, had generated a high demand for foodstuffs. The stagnant agricultural sector was not even coming close to meeting this demand and the territory was importing most of its food. Planners hoped to revitalize local agricultural production as a substitute for these imports, and indeed between 1960 and 1970 market production (of fruits, vegetables, livestock, and fish) increased threefold; however, imports of these items increased twice as fast as local production (Blanchet 1984:40).

Looking to the future, officials realized that the completion of the CEP at the end of the decade would generate a large contingent of urban unemployed (about 3,000 jobs would be lost) used to high salaries and inflated living standards. They realized as well that the economy, even allowing for the hoped-for growth in tourism and light industry, could not absorb these soon-to-be unemployed wage earners. Thus, planners hoped to promote commercial agriculture as well as copra production, fishing, and other market-oriented activities in rural areas, thereby providing rural employment. To get off the ground and remain viable, these projects have required substantial subsidies from the government.

It was also hoped that new rural economic opportunities would encourage islanders to stay and work in the outer islands. The government set aside special funds to provide financial aid to urban families willing to repatriate to their outer-island homes.

The Tuamotu islands, the major producers of copra, were targeted for the development of copra production, while the Austral chain of southerly islands with temperate climates (mainly the island of Tubuai) was targeted for the development of European vegetable cash-cropping (see Thompson and Adloff 1971; Connell 1985). The Society Islands of Moorea and Huahine would emerge as major melon and pineapple producers, respectively. With the exception of copra, destined for the Papeete mill and eventually to be exported as oil, agricultural production was aimed at meeting local Papeete market demand.

In addition to the creation of these new economic opportunities, improvements in social services and infrastructure (including much-needed social welfare programs, provided in part by various French entitlement programs) were critical components of rural development strategies. In the 1960s, the small number of available social services in the territory, including schools and clinics, were concentrated on Tahiti and virtually absent on outer islands. In 1967, for example, the territory as a whole possessed only two high schools, both located in Papeete.

Starting in the 1960s and continuing to the present, new schools, clinics, government buildings, roads, airstrips, and other modern amenities have been constructed in rural areas and on outer islands. Many of these islands were also electrified for the first time in the 1980s.

Even the most remote Tahitian outer island has felt the impact of government-sponsored, regional modernization programs, including the introduction of French-style education and health care, French radio and television programs, French entitlement programs, and French "development." Not only has the pace of Westernization accelerated, but Tahitian assimilation to French culture and values has been achieved to a degree that could not have been predicted in earlier decades.

Footing the Bill

Funding for regional development and social programs comes predominantly from French taxpayers. Islanders pay no income taxes and the territorial budget is funded mainly through French aid/military payments and customs duties. In 1981, France gave approximately $400 million of aid (about 40,000 million CFP) to the territory (*Europa World Yearbook* 1985). By 1986, that amount had risen to $500 million or $2,250 per capita (Crocombe 1987:238), one of the highest per capita levels of aid to any developing nation. (Henningham [1989a:110] estimates that the territory received $770 million in French aid in 1986.)

Military expenditures are a major part of total French government spending in the region. In 1981, the CEP itself accounted for about 30 percent of all territorial revenues (Breeze 1981:31). In 1986, military spending constituted approximately 60 percent of all government spending in

France's Pacific territories (Henningham 1989a:100). While these funds represent only a small proportion of the total French national budget (less than 1 percent according to Aldrich and Connell 1988), they have played a pivotal role in institutionalizing aid dependency and in solidifying the French presence in the islands.

France has recently agreed to invest even more development-oriented funds to promote greater economic self-reliance in the territory. Some French officials foresee a time when nuclear testing may wind down, leading to reductions in military payments to the territory. Moreover, if regional development takes hold or, in other words, if productivity increases and if the territory can thereby become more self-supporting, France hopes that its financial burden will be lessened. However, the extent to which self-reliance can be generated by steadily mounting infusions of French aid and heavily subsidized (and non-self-supporting) development programs remains to be seen.

▲ Welfare State Colonialism

The funds the territory receives in the form of aid, subsidies, and loans are an integral part of local financing for government services and for development programs. Such investment and expansion of the public sector generates a significant number of salaried government jobs for islanders. As secure and well-paying government jobs have become available, islanders' participation in primary productive activities (agriculture, fishing, crafts, etc.) has declined and importation has increased. On many rural outer islands, in particular, government employment is the major source of cash income.

Islanders' relatively high standard of living is also maintained by cash they receive from various French entitlement programs, including the family allocation system and elderly pension/retirement system. Their incomes are further inflated through their access to heavily subsidized development projects (in cash-cropping or copra plantation development).

Regional modernization programs have also brought free education, health care, and other social services to all of the islands of the territory. As a result, islanders' standard of social welfare is quite high, even compared to the Western industrialized nations. Tahitian islanders have become dependent on French funds for their jobs, social services, and an inflated standard of living, which they would be unable to achieve on their own.

In sum, these processes generate a neocolonial dependency relationship and artificial prosperity—welfare state colonialism. Through its implementation in French Polynesia, France has been able to generate a certain amount of goodwill toward its continuing presence and to solidify political ties that islanders would be able to sever only at great cost to themselves.

Tubuai Prosperity

Perhaps more than any other outer island, Tubuai has been a particular target of government development and, as a result, has experienced the full brunt of French-style modernization. Prior to the 1960s, Tubuai was like other rural outer islands in that it was largely isolated from the mainstream of activity on Tahiti. Although an occasional cargo ship or trading schooner from Papeete dropped anchor bringing imported goods and news from Tahiti, islanders made their living as subsistence-oriented taro farmers and fishermen. Tubuaians were able to sell (and more often barter) small amounts of copra, manioc starch, coffee, and fresh foods to these ships, receiving canned foods, sugar, kerosene, and cloth in exchange.

In the late 1950s, the government's big push for regional development and modernization began. Because Tubuai possessed a temperate climate and abundant agricultural lands, it was selected for the development of commercial agriculture. Various heavily subsidized development programs were implemented whose aim was to turn the island's taro farmers into cultivators of European vegetables. These would be exported to Papeete markets to help meet growing market demand. By the late 1980s, Tubuai would be exporting over 1,200 tons of potatoes and several hundred tons of carrots and other vegetables to Papeete each year.

Although successful, vegetable cultivation and export on Tubuai are heavily dependent on government subsidies, price supports, financial aids, and other infrastructural supports. Without these supports, Tubuai produce would not be able to compete with less expensive foreign imports, nor would Tubuai farmers have the wherewithal (capital, technology, etc.) to participate in the project. Clearly, Tubuai vegetable production is not, at present, economically self-sustaining. Nevertheless, islanders have financially benefited from this development opportunity and many families' incomes have risen as a result of their participation.

In an administrative reorganization in the early 1960s, Tubuai was also designated as the administrative center for the newly constituted Austral Islands subdivision of the territory. As a new regional government center, offices of government service agencies were set up on the island. These included the Austral Islands administration, territorial public works (Travaux Publiques), an agricultural service, a school system, an Austral Islands clinic, and so on. In 1972, a small airstrip was built and flights (government subsidized) began arriving from Papeete twice a week.

With the arrival of the Austral Islands administration and government services, jobs were created for islanders. For the most part, they were employed by a greatly expanded public sector to provide services to themselves. By 1987, there were approximately 190 jobs on the island, about 90 percent of which were government-sponsored employment. About half of all island families today include a wage-earning member, and government salaries are by far the major source of income on the island.

Islanders were also integrated into the territory's family welfare system (Caisse de la Prévoyance Sociale), and they began to receive child welfare payments (*allocations familiales*). In the early 1980s, islanders were also integrated into the government's retirement pension system; this provides monthly stipends to those over the age of 60. Tubuaians also have access to free French education and medical care.

New jobs and cash-earning opportunities in agriculture have substantially raised islanders' incomes, creating a prosperity that would have been unimaginable earlier. In 1987, the average familial income was about $12,000 a year. Imported foods are now an important component of islanders' diets, and Western consumer/luxury goods long ago replaced indigenous crafts and household items.

Takapoto Prosperity

The atoll of Takapoto in the Tuamotu archipelago has felt the impact of welfare state colonialism in a slightly different way. Throughout the 1960s and early 1970s, this tiny impoverished atoll lost much of its population through emigration to Papeete; in 1970 the inhabitants numbered only ninety. The atoll itself possesses few resources and its population had always earned a marginal living through copra production.

Major changes took place in the 1970s, however—changes that would raise islanders' standard of living, bring them into close contact with Papeete, and trigger a flow of return migration to the atoll (Pollock 1978, 1979; Robineau 1977). Most important, the government raised and subsidized the price of copra (to 30CFP/kg—about $0.40/kg) as one part of a plan to develop Tuamotu copra production. In addition, a branch of the Service de la Pêche (fisheries service) was brought to the island and it began to develop a pearl culture operation on the atoll. Islanders, organized into a pearling cooperative, could earn money gathering oysters, which would then be grafted by a Japanese specialist to produce pearls. With their earnings from copra and pearls, islanders were constructing new houses and purchasing major imported consumer items. The government also constructed a small airstrip on the atoll that began to receive several flights each week from Papeete; this gave islanders access to education, health care, and other services in the city.

Although there is no information available on the atoll in the 1980s, the population's standard of living has undoubtedly continued to rise. Even in the late 1970s, most islanders owned electric generators, washing machines, and lawnmowers (Pollock 1978). Islanders are also now participating in the territory's various government entitlement programs. The economic opportunities and standard of living are such that in recent years the atoll has attracted a wave of return migration.

With the exception of government employment opportunities, the situations of Takapoto and Tubuai are similar in many ways. In both cases, government-subsidized development programs, as well as entitlement programs, are sustaining a standard of living that islanders would be unable to achieve on their own.

Pollock (1978) compares the standard of living on Takapoto with that of Namu, an atoll in the Marshall Islands that was administered directly by the United States at the time she studied it in the 1970s. In size and resource endowment, the atolls are much alike, and both populations depend primarily on copra to make their living. The similarity, however, ends there. On Namu, islanders live in poverty. The price of copra was only about $0.06/kg in the early 1970s (compared to Takapoto's subsidized $0.40/kg). There were no other cash-earning options and islanders lived a largely subsistence-based lifestyle in which they produced most of their own food and other necessities. Contacts with other islands were limited, as they relied on the sporadic visits of occasional cargo ships. In contrast, the people of Takapoto visited Papeete often and were increasingly dependent on imports; three general stores served the small population. Pollock (1978) concludes that French government programs are responsible for generating the Takapoto population's current high standard of living. Without them, life on Takapoto would be much like life on Namu.

▲ *Autonomie Interne:* Local Self-Government

Although the territory was becoming ever more mired in financial and political dependence on France during the 1970s and 1980s, Tahitians were nevertheless demanding a greater say in their own affairs. Feeling pressure from the growing Third World decolonization movement led by the United Nations, as well as pressure from growing pan–Pacific island nation condemnation of its nuclear testing program, France acquiesced to islanders' demands. By French government acts in 1977 and 1984, the territory was granted *autonomie interne* (local self-government), which included greater control by the Territorial Assembly of the territorial budget and development planning.

France, however, retains control over external affairs, including critical areas such as defense, higher education, and justice. Although the president of the locally elected Territorial Assembly is now officially designated as the region's chief executive, the French high commissioner continues in many ways to be its effective governor. In short, France has maintained a significant degree of control over territorial affairs and, since it holds the purse strings, continues to play a major role in dictating the course of events in its political satellite.

The granting of local self-government has been associated with an easing of France's previously strict assimilationist policies in the territory and its adoption of a more "bicultural view" (Henningham 1992:147). Starting in the early 1980s, the requirement that children speak only French in public schools was changed to allow the use of Tahitian as well. Whereas French had been the official language of the territory, Tahitian was granted the status of joint official language; today Tahitian, not French, is the major language used by the largely bilingual delegates to the Territorial Assembly. And the French government has also recently allowed the Tahitian (preannexation) flag to be flown next to the French tricolor in front of public buildings and on ceremonial occasions.

Despite a well-developed desire for local political autonomy, pro-independence sentiments among the Tahitian population have virtually disappeared. Only 15 to 20 percent of the present electorate supports various political parties that seek independence and oppose nuclear testing (Henningham 1989a:109). Even the most outspoken leaders of the Tahitian autonomists have mellowed with time. As one such leader, Francis Sanford, concluded, "Our education is French. We are used to French development. Our money is backed by France. If we have a piece of land, a home and a job, that is more important than independence" (quoted in *Pacific Islands Monthly* 1980). One must conclude that welfare state colonialism has proven to be a particularly effective strategy for both undermining pro-independence agitation and permanently cementing ties between France and French Polynesia.

▲ The MIRAB Nations of the South Pacific

In the basic parameters of its dependent economic and political situation, French Polynesia resembles many other Pacific island societies. Most Pacific island microstates share the same set of constraints, including small population size, distances from markets, limited resources and development potential, and ongoing dependency on present or former colonial masters. Consequently, a number of important parallels in their contemporary statuses can be identified.

Bertram and Watters (1985) have characterized the microstates of the South Pacific as having MIRAB economies: economies based on substantial out-*migration* and financial dependence on *remittances* from overseas wage earners, reliance on overseas *aid* supplied by various metropolitan powers (usually the previous colonizer) to maintain government services, and a large government *bureaucracy* (financed by aid) as the major local employer. It is in the small, economically marginal, and politically independent nations of the Cook Islands, Niue, Tokelau (still a territory of New Zealand), Tuvalu, and Kiribati that the MIRAB phenomenon is most entrenched. In others, including Tonga, Western Samoa, and American Samoa, dependence on overseas aid is well established (see Crocombe 1987), as are patterns of out-migration and remittance dependency.

The constellation of factors that make up the MIRAB package reflect on the one hand the limited economic options open to these remote and resource-poor islands, and on the other hand the ongoing desire of the metropolitan powers to maintain (despite decolonization) an active military/strategic presence in the islands. Thus, many nominally independent island nations accept substantial aid payments—the extension of the metropolitan welfare state—in exchange for the continuing presence of their former colonial masters.

Relative to other areas of the Third World, the islands of the South Pacific have been described as "conspicuously successful" in attracting foreign aid. This success can be attributed to the enduring geopolitical interests of the major powers in the region: Australia, New Zealand, France, the United States, and Great Britain (Bertram and Watters 1985:513). While interests are diverse, Western nations have mainly sought the strategic use of islands for military installations and port facilities. In this regard, the islands have long been a buffer zone between the Eastern powers (particularly Japan and the Soviet Union) and the West. The United States, of course, has maintained its extensive military/strategic presence in the Micronesian islands since the end of World War II.

In the 1970s and early 1980s, some analysts argued that if the Western powers declined to furnish aid to needy Pacific nations, the Soviet Union would move in quickly to fill the gap, thereby gaining a strategic foothold in the Pacific long denied to it. Considering the recent political splintering of the Soviet Union and the severe internal problems presently besieging its former constituent republics, such concern appears now to be ill-founded. Exactly how the recent warming of Cold War politics will affect the strategic interests of the world powers in the region—including Japan—is not yet clear, although it may substantially undermine the islands' ability to attract overseas aid.

There is also growing interest among Western nations, as well as Japan, in exploiting the potentially rich marine resources of the Pacific Ocean basin. Such resources include fish, seabed minerals, and possibly petroleum. If this were to materialize, the 200-mile exclusive economic zones that surround each island nation may become valuable economic collateral, bestowing on these tiny nations greater economic and political clout in the world system at large.

External Dependency

For many island nations, aid payments maintain the relatively high levels of government services and salaries (jobs/bureaucracy) first established during the colonial era. Islanders have become accustomed to modern services such as Western health care, education, communications, and utilities. In addition, because employment and other economic opportunities are limited on home islands, metropolitan powers frequently facilitate out-migration to their own urban centers (by providing work permits, visas, etc.), where islanders find work usually as unskilled labor. For example, a large number of islanders from the Cooks and Niue, both self-governing states in "free association" with New Zealand, now reside and work in Auckland.

While the MIRAB phenomenon does sustain a relatively high standard of living and social welfare in many poor island nations, one can argue that it not only generates dependency on the metropolitan power, but also it directly promotes island underdevelopment and import dependency. Out-migration, remittance dependency, and access to subsidized employment in the public sector all displace labor from primary economic production, predominantly agriculture, in these nations. Moreover, families remaining on home islands come to depend on remittances sent by employed kin for a substantial portion of their cash incomes, and primary production declines further. These salaries and remittances, unlike earnings from less remunerative agriculture, provide islanders with the income required to meet their inflated consumption standards, particularly of expensive Western imports (clothing, cars, trucks, stereos, etc.)

Despite the prevalence of such conditions, it is nevertheless the expressed goal of many of the new nation states of the Pacific to achieve self-sustaining economic growth. This is reflected in island governments' optimistic development goals. Bertram (1986) offers a pessimistic commentary on such optimism, however, arguing that idealistic development planning in these nations is misguided (and probably doomed to failure) precisely because the MIRAB phenomenon *is* the economy. These economies are "driven by rents rather than by income from productive export-oriented activities" (Bertram 1986:810). Because they lack true development potential, he proposes that the most viable development option for these microstates is the maintenance of the MIRAB package; the "sustainability of . . . [islanders'] living standards . . . hinges upon the durability of existing and future sources of rent income" (Bertram 1986:810).

It is unlikely that the MIRAB phenomenon, or the neocolonial relations of dependency associated with it, is a transient feature of the political economies of Pacific island states. Instead, there is every reason to believe that it will continue to be the economy for decades to come.

In light of the experiences of other Third World nations, one might wonder to what extent Pacific islanders' neocolonial dependency generates ill feelings or hostility to the ever-present Western nations. The evidence suggests that relations in the Pacific between island and metropolitan nations are generally amiable and agreeable to all parties (see Crocombe 1987). Part of that amiability can be attributed to the fact that, in most cases, it was the colonizers themselves (Britain, New Zealand, and Australia) who actively moved their island possessions toward self-government. No major anticolonial movement has ever successfully coalesced in the Pacific (Crocombe 1987), with the possible recent exception of volatile New Caledonia.

Western nations are also responsible for introducing the democratic institutions upon which island societies are building their new nation states. And finally, Western nations are the cultural and spiritual homelands of the Christian religious sects with which many islanders identify. In many ways, then, the cultural and political affiliations between island nations and the metropolitan powers who subsidize them are strong.

The perspective of the new Pacific island states appears to be well summarized in Crocombe's (1987:197) pragmatic assessment of the situation: "Nobody is independent today, and the crucial issue is what extent of dependence is considered acceptable, or inevitable, in what area of life, at what costs, weighed against what benefits."

▲ France in the Pacific

The strong parallels between the way France has intervened in French Polynesia and how other Western nations have intervened in the Pacific microstates attached to them are clearly evident. The most important of these parallels is the extension of the metropolitan welfare state to island society, the extensive dependence on aid to subsidize the territorial budget and provide government services, and the maintenance of a large public sector (financed by aid) that is the major employer of islanders. The consequences of these policies, notably ever-declining primary production, an escalating trade deficit and import dependency, and artificially inflated consumption standards, also characterize both French Polynesia and the other Pacific microstates.

The situation in the Micronesian islands resembles that of French Polynesia in many ways (see Kiste 1993; McHenry 1975; Peoples 1978). Although the United States has allowed the island groups of the former trust territory to move toward independence, it has also sought to retain its military installations and strategic base of influence there. Both the Marshall Islands and the Federated States of Micronesia, for example, are now "independent in free association" with the United States. In exchange for its military bases and ongoing political influence over the islands, the United States will transfer about $2.5 billion to them over the next fifteen years. The funds will support extensive government employment for islanders, as well as various government services and development programs (Kiste 1993)—in short, an inflated standard of living.

As islanders have become dependent on government employment and transfer payments, primary production has declined and importation has soared in the new Micronesian states. In the late 1980s, Marshall Islanders were importing 92 percent of their food. The islands produce very little and depend almost entirely on U.S. funding to support their standard of living. The only major difference between French Polynesia and these Micronesian states is that the former is a heavily dependent "colony," while the latter are heavily dependent, unofficial "colonies."

Unlike the other Western powers in the region, France directly controls its Pacific possessions, while elsewhere island states practice a substantially greater degree of internal political self-determination. Even in its gradual transfer of local self-government to French Polynesia, France has lagged far behind other Western powers.

Another major difference between France and the other Western nations is that it "has been both willing and able to invest substantial sums in rural development, and the availability of comparable levels of funding in most [Pacific island nations] is more limited" (Connell 1985:50). Rural development that emphasizes growth in agriculture and aquaculture has been an important cornerstone of territorial economic development and modernization strategies. Moreover, as Connell (1985:50) notes, "Problems of urbanization [as well as other regional economic problems] are viewed as being minimized primarily by development of rural areas and remote archipelagoes, rather than through the improvement of urban amenities and the generation of urban employment." In contrast, other Pacific island nations have relied heavily on international migration and repatriated remittances to sustain their fragile economies.

Another significant difference is that, unlike in many Pacific microstates (e.g., Samoa, Tonga, and the Cooks, just to mention a few), international migration from French Polynesia has been negligible. Nowhere else in the Pacific have development strategies aimed directly at population retention, preventing rural-urban migration, and encouraging return rural migration (by providing financial aid to returnees) been implemented (Connell 1985). Recent evidence suggests that these strategies are indeed working (Pollock 1978; Lockwood 1990). Of course, France has assumed the not insignificant financial burden associated with these programs.

In recent years, France has also deliberately pursued a higher profile in Pacific affairs at large (Henningham 1989b; 1992). Hoping to contain, mute, and otherwise undermine growing antinuclear and prodecolonization agitation by Pacific island nations, France has extended overseas aid to a number of them (see Henningham 1989a:120). Some of the projects it has funded most recently include postcyclone reconstruction in the Cook Islands, the construction of theaters, schools, and airstrips in Western Samoa, and the building of a stadium in Tonga for the 1989 South Pacific games (Henningham 1989a:115). Significant packets of direct French aid to Fiji, Vanuatu, and some of the Micronesian islands were also initiated in the 1980s. While other Western powers, including the United States, Australia, and New Zealand, are active aid-donors in the region, France differs from the others in that it pursues this policy, at least in part, to generate goodwill to its active nuclear and neocolonial presence in the region.

PART 2

Rural Tahitian Society
and Capitalism

▲ 5
Tubuai Modernization:
Linkages and Dependency

The many changes that started to take place in the Tahitian islands in the early 1960s—the building of the nuclear testing complex, territorial economic development and the growth of tourism, and the implementation of French welfare state colonialism—fully integrated Tahitian society into the French state and world capitalist system. That integration has brought new opportunities and constraints into Tahitians' lives and laid the groundwork for fundamental cultural and organizational changes in island society.

Today, most of the Tahitian population resides in the Papeete urban center, having chosen to abandon rural life on the outer islands. Even the more traditional lifestyle of the outer islands now almost always includes wage jobs or the production of export commodities. Unlike their grandparents, who struggled to barter copra for a few nails and bolts of cloth, Tahitians today are affluent. And even though Tahitians have a strong sense of their own ethnic identity, that identity reflects Tahitians' increasing Western assimilation and affiliation.

The integration of Tahitian society into the world system required the creation (and maintenance) of critical structural linkages between Tahitian communities, the French state, and the world at large. In the process of economically developing the region and extending the French welfare state to the islands, the French government has been responsible for organizing and financing most of these major linkages.

Some of the islands' linkages are administrative and political, geared to physically incorporating Tahitian communities into the French state and consolidating them into one territorial political entity. Other linkages are economic, aimed at making it possible for Tahitian producers to participate in capitalist markets—both as exporters of their agricultural commodities and consumers of the manufactured goods of the industrialized nations. Still other linkages are cultural, aimed at bringing the "benefits" of Western and French civilization to Tahitian society by exposing it to Western education, Western media, and Western medicine.

Tubuai's airport (photo: Lockwood)

The resources—some material and some immaterial—that flow through these linkages generate the strategic economic, political, and social interdependencies that now connect Tahitian society to the rest of the world. From France (and in some cases, other parts of the world) come money (salaries, subsidies, transfer payments), development programs, technology, information, imported consumer goods, and Western "culture." Tahitian society offers a small number of various export commodities on world markets. But Tahitians also transfer an important intangible resource to France: their political clientage and cultural affiliation.

By examining the nature of Tubuai's structural linkages, particularly the content, volume, relative valuation, and direction of resource flow, one can learn a great deal about precisely how Tahitian society is integrated into the French state and world system. More specifically, one can gain important insights into Tubuai's role in the regional and international division of labor (in the world capitalist economy); into its neocolonial, politically subordinate relationship with the French state and its financial dependency on it; and into the nature of its social and cultural ties with France and other Western nations. Because these linkages structure the economic, political, and social opportunities available to islanders today, they play an important role in shaping the Neo-Tahitian society of the 1990s.

▲ Administrative Linkages and Political Integration

One of the things that first strikes the visitor to Tubuai and many of the other remote outer islands of French Polynesia is just how unisolated they are. The long arm of French welfare state colonialism has reached out to embrace and incorporate each and every island community, no matter how distant or small. This has been accomplished through the creation of a highly effective administrative and political system (centered in Papeete and Paris), which directs the flow of government resources (revenues, programs, and so on) to all of the far-flung communities in the territory.

Tahitian Society and the French State

As an overseas territory of France, the Tahitian islands have become fully incorporated into the French state, and various French administrative, governmental, and political structures operate within the territory. But the state is present in numerous other ways as well; some are symbolic and ceremonial, while others reflect the French state's active export of French culture to its overseas dependencies.

Despite their territorial status, Tahitians are French citizens with all of the rights and duties that implies. They vote (by universal adult suffrage) in all major French elections and are represented by two elected deputies to the French National Assembly in Paris and one representative in the French Senate. They also elect representatives to their own Territorial Assembly.

Major French government officials as well as candidates running for offices in France frequently travel to the territory hoping to garner support and votes. In the late 1980s, for example, François Mitterrand, the president of France, not only visited Papeete, but also spent time on some of the outer islands, including Tubuai's neighbor Rurutu.

Tahitians are politically active and even on the outer islands many belong to the territory's various political parties (Henningham 1992:156–157). Many of these parties have direct affiliations with political parties in France. Most Tubuaians belong to one of the two conservative parties that now dominate the Territorial Assembly, Te Tiarama (The Torch) and Tahoeraa Huiraatira (Rally of the People). Both favor continuing strong links to France. In general, outer islanders are known for their relative political conservatism; the small socialist, anti–nuclear testing, and pro-independence parties have their largest followings among urban Tahitians (Papeete).

In addition to governmental structures and the ever-present French bureaucracy, there are many ways in which the French state is an active part of Tubuai islanders' lives. France is in direct control of secondary education, legal affairs/police, and medical care on the island. The state finances and runs the island's high school, Collège d'Enseignement Secondaire (CES), sending French teachers to staff it. It also sends military *gendarmes* to the island to keep social order and to oversee legal affairs (e.g., land transfers). These *gendarmes* represent the authority of state; the island's five Tahitian policemen (*mutoi*) mostly do odd jobs for the municipality and have little authority. And France sends a French doctor and dentist to the island to provide medical care.

As French citizens, young Tahitian men are required to perform one year of compulsory duty with the French military (usually at age 18). While most Tubuai men perform their service at one of the military bases in or near Papeete, a few serve at bases in France. Many of these young men send photos home to their families showing themselves either in uniform on a busy French boulevard or knee-deep in snow with arms around a young French girlfriend. Although it is not unusual for Tahitians to want to stay in France after their service, they find it difficult to find work with their limited job skills and sometimes limited French language skills; most return.

Tubuaians are also symbolically reminded of their political affiliation with France on Bastille Day, July 14, when the French tricolor is ceremonially raised on the flagpole in front of the town hall, the *mairie*. Following this ceremony, the island's school children sing the Marseillaise, the French national anthem, in front of a large group of assembled spectators.

After a presentation of songs for visiting government officials celebrating the July 14th festival, members of a Tubuai women's craft association attend a feast in the officials' honor (photo: Lance Rasbridge).

Bastille Day, the day marking the overthrow of the French monarchy and establishment of the French Republic, is the major holiday celebrated throughout the territory. A grand *fête* that lasts for several weeks is held in Papeete to commemorate the event each year. It includes a lavish Tahitian dance competition, traditional Tahitian games and tests of strength, sports events, and a huge street festival; it attracts tourists from around the world. The preservation of traditional Tahitian dances, crafts, and foods and their display at this festival are actively supported by various government agencies.

Territorial Administration and Local Government

Although the French high commissioner holds ultimate power in the territory, the locally elected Territorial Assembly has increasingly played a major role in internal affairs since the implementation of *autonomie interne*. At that time, territorial agencies took over a number of the administrative duties previously performed by French state agencies.

The territorial government is run largely by the forty-one-member Territorial Assembly. Each island group, or administrative subdivision, elects representatives to it. Tubuai is the administrative center of the five Austral Islands, which as a unit sends two representatives.

The Assembly elects from among its members a territorial president, who then chooses and presides over an executive body, the Council of Ministers. After the French high commissioner, the president of the territory is the next most powerful figure in the region. The territorial ministers are also powerful, each overseeing one area such as education, economic and social development, agriculture, health, and so on.

The important unit of local-level community government is the *Commune,* or municipality. The French commune system was first established on all of the islands in the territory in 1972. This system's extension beyond Papeete was aimed at increasing local participation in government and bringing much-needed government services to the outer islands. As Henningham (1992:135–136) notes, it "also provided further support to the French presence . . . by encouraging communities to be more aware that the funding for improvements to infrastructure and services came from France."

The island of Tubuai is its own municipal commune, the Commune de Tubuai, and it elects an island mayor who controls the island budget. That budget is funded by allocations from the Territorial Assembly. An elected municipal council of about fifteen members advises the mayor and approves the budget. Tubuai is also divided into three administrative subcommunes (districts), each of which elects an adjunct mayor who serves on the island's municipal council.

The Municipal Budget, Government Jobs, and the Flow of Money

Tubuai's municipal budget is one of the major channels through which governmental resources flow directly to the island. The municipality is the single largest employer, and the budget pays the salaries of these employees. In addition, the municipal budget also provides funds for the administrative affairs of the island, for the upkeep of buildings and schools, for the installation of electricity, and for certain categories of social aid. In 1980, Tubuai's budget totaled approximately $1,050,000, although the mayor had access to supplemental funds on occasion. By 1987, it had increased to about $2,200,000; this included approximately $400,000 specifically earmarked for electrification.

In addition to municipal jobs, islanders are employed by various territorial and state government agencies on the island, including the public works service (Travaux Publiques), the agricultural service (Service de l'Économie Rurale), the primary and high schools, and the health clinic. There are about 190 jobs on the island; 92 percent of these are government jobs.

As noted above, islanders are mostly employed to supply various government services to themselves. Most of these jobs are unskilled— islanders regravel the road or repair bridges, cook lunches or serve as janitors in the primary schools, or plant trees and load potato sacks for the agricultural service. There are a few skilled positions: school-teachers, electricians, masons, administrators, and so on. Minimum wage levels are set by the government, and in 1987 the average worker earned about $700–$800 a month. That same worker earned $400 a month in 1981. About half (54 percent) of all island households include an employed member.

The government is the major employer on the island not only because it operates numerous agencies and services, but also because private sector employment is virtually nonexistent. On Tubuai there are no small businesses or other private enterprises (no restaurants, hotels, etc.). The island's two Chinese family-operated stores are the only retail commerce, and they monopolize all commercial activities. Both rely predominantly on their own familial labor to run their stores, although each employs several islanders. Other than the general stores, there is a branch of Air Tahiti and a branch of a Tahiti bank; each employs one or two islanders.

Tubuai men hold 73 percent of all jobs on the island and, with the exception of teaching and secretarial positions, dominate positions requiring job-related skills. In addition to working as teachers and secretaries, a few Tubuai women have obtained jobs as cooks, janitors (cleaning personnel), and teachers' aides. One exceptional Tubuai woman who graduated from the territorial agricultural school now works for the independent agency that runs the Tubuai potato project.

Political Patronage, Resources, and Power

Public officials are extremely powerful in the territory because they control the resources that flow from the government to local communities. All government agencies, and thus virtually all employment (and salaries), are under the ultimate control of municipal, territorial, and state (France) officials. Moreover, the operation of all social services—health, education, development programs, the installation of electricity, land records, and so on—is controlled by these officials. It would be fair to say that beyond the familial/household level, almost everything on Tubuai is run by the government.

Islanders attempt to manipulate their access to the power of particular local and territorial officials by developing highly personalistic ties to them. And in this relatively small territory where everyone knows everyone else, political patronage is one of the dominant features of regional politics. Indeed, "political careers are founded on the ability to provide patronage" (Henningham 1992:153).

For their part, officials are willing to exchange their influence/brokerage for support from individuals and families during elections. Officials can help islanders find government jobs and extend the brokerage power of their offices to help them negotiate the cumbersome bureaucracy that pervades most spheres of life in the islands. Islanders are quick to say that one can expect little help from an official who is not of one's own political party and with whom one has not developed a personalistic tie. Those islanders belonging to parties not in power frequently complain that rampant favoritism and corruption characterize the distribution of government benefits and services.

The development of political patronage ties between Tubuai islanders and government officials takes place both when islanders travel to Papeete and when officials come to the islands. When territorial and state government officials visit Tubuai, they are greeted lavishly at the airport and bedecked with flower and shell *hei's* (necklaces). A large feast, usually put on by the local members of the officials' political party, is also prepared to honor the visitors.

During these visits, a public forum is usually convened at the *mairie* (town hall), in which officials speak and islanders voice their views and grievances. Most commonly, islanders express their concerns over high prices and ever-increasing inflation. They also complain about what they consider to be insufficient government allocations to Tubuai for much-needed electricity and road repairs (the island has only one road), as well as alleged government mismanagement of various sorts, including the purchase of a new Austral Islands cargo ship in the mid-1980s that was unable to navigate Tubuai's shallow lagoon and tie up at the new wharf. The discussion ranges from the mundane—the cost of staple foods under government price controls at the Chinese-operated general stores—to the philosophical—the French presence versus independence. These typically volatile and highly partisan public meetings usually last hours into the night.

The next day, visiting officials meet with individuals who come to solicit their support for personal matters. A woman may approach an Australs representative or territorial minister, for example, complaining that her husband was never paid his vacation pay by the public works service and asking that her grievance be personally investigated by the official. Or a farmer may ask an official to intervene on his behalf so that his application for an agricultural subsidy might be granted.

Gender and Politics

Tahitian women are virtually absent from positions of political leadership at both the territorial and local community levels. Until recently, the members of the Territorial Assembly, Council of Ministers, and local island councils were all male. In 1991, a woman was named to be the new territorial minister of agriculture, causing confusion, consternation, and rampant speculation about possible implications among the workers at Tubuai's agricultural service. Although this appointment may reflect increasing political opportunities for women in the territory, the political domain in Tahitian society is heavily male dominated.

Tahitian women do vote in elections and are actively vocal in political meetings. And like men, they work to manipulate the political patronage system in order to achieve particular goals or acquire specific benefits from the system.

The major difference in women's and men's participation in the patronage system is that women's is more limited. It is men who hold most government jobs and who are directly involved in most government development programs and bureaucratic affairs. The two major exceptions to this are women's control of family welfare benefits and their participation in government-sponsored craft associations. Women will approach public officials on personal or familial matters (as in the example described above), on matters related to receipt of their family allocations, or on craft association business.

In her study of women's craft associations in Papeete, Jones (1991) describes at length how Papeete women solicit the patronage of the local mayor and other officials in order to receive benefits for their associations (use of the *mairie* or other public buildings for association functions, acquisition of government subsidies, and so on). In exchange, craft association members support the official during elections by soliciting votes, passing out campaign buttons, or organizing *fêtes* on his behalf.

▲ Government Social Services and Welfare Programs

Entitlement Programs

In addition to government revenues received through salaried employment, islanders also receive money through various entitlement programs. The two programs that touch virtually every islander are family allocations and the pension system.

All families with children, regardless of income, receive child welfare allocations of approximately $55 a month per child. These allocations, paid by the Caisse de la Prévoyance Sociale based in Papeete, are meant to promote the well-being of children (nutrition, clothing, etc.). While pregnant, a woman can receive additional subsidies.

Family allocations are now paid directly to women, although until recently they were paid to male heads of families. According to islanders, the policy changed when it was realized that the funds would have the highest probability of being used for their intended purpose if they were given directly to mothers. Islanders say this is best because it is women who take care of the family's food and clothing needs, and because some men have been known to squander family allocations on drinking and gambling. (These are considered to be "male" activities, in which very few island women participate.) Today the average Tubuai family receives $100–$200 per month in allocations.

Islanders also become eligible to receive government retirement pensions at age 60. The retirement pensions of government employees are financed by regular deductions from their paychecks. Nonformally employed islanders, the bulk of Tubuai's farmers and fishermen, can now also receive retirement pensions. A new program, instituted in the early 1980s, allows such individuals, both male and female, to declare themselves "employed" in agriculture (cash-crop or subsistence), fishing, or craft production and thus eligible for a pension. Tubuai retirees receive between $300 and $1,000 a month from the government.

Formal Education

Today, the territorial government is responsible for primary education and the state (France) for secondary education. By exporting the French educational system to the islands, France has attempted to promote cultural assimilation. But once implanted in French Polynesia, the system has proven to be only minimally successful. High rates of student failure and dropping out have minimized the impact French education might have had on islanders.

Studies of the educational system on Tubuai suggest that the curriculum is frequently culturally inappropriate and that Tahitian styles of learning are significantly different from those found in Western societies (Levin 1978;

Perrin 1978). In addition, France's (pre-1980) insistence that students speak only French in school (and that they go by a French name) also contributed to high rates of failure among them.

Even today, most young people on Tubuai have attended only five or six years of primary school, and few hold a certificate of having finished. The French civil code states that school attendance is mandatory until the age of 14 and many young people (often still in primary school) leave at that age. Older islanders have usually attended only one or two years of primary school, and many do not read or write well, in either Tahitian or French.

Nevertheless, the educational system does expose Tahitian students to the world beyond the islands and to Western role models, values, and worldview. When asked, for instance, to write an essay about what they would like to be when they grow up, the vast majority of Tubuai students described goals of becoming a doctor, lawyer, or teacher; many young girls wanted to become *couturières* (dress designers) (Levin and Lockwood 1984). While students have clearly absorbed Western ideas about prestigious occupations, the likelihood of their achieving these goals is virtually nil. For those who remain on the island (as most young people of the 1990s will), making a living may include a wage job (unskilled, minimum wage), but it will most likely center on farming and fishing, the mainstays of the island economy.

The few students who do succeed in the local school system often go to Papeete to attend various vocational schools. The top students have the opportunity to attend universities in France through government scholarships. Plans are now under way to build the territory's first university in Papeete.

By creating aspirations of Western lifestyles, the educational system has played a role in making cash earning a major priority in Tubuai families and thus in promoting local economic development. But by instilling aspirations that will probably never be achieved, it has also promoted frustration and discontent among young people. I was surprised in 1991 to learn of the recent suicides of three young people; these were the first mentions of suicide I had heard since starting fieldwork on the island in 1980. Everyone agreed that young people today are under numerous kinds of stress, many of which are linked to the difficulties of finding jobs and earning (enough) money.

Television Reception

While the French educational system attempts to play a central role in promoting Tahitians' cultural assimilation to Western society, television has proven to be a much more effective agent of acculturation. Indeed, most of what islanders know of the world has been gleaned from U.S. and French television shows. Before the government's recent construction of an antenna to allow reception of television broadcasts directly from Papeete, the municipal government broadcast shows it received on cassette tapes for two hours each evening. In addition to the U.S., French, and British movies shown on television, islanders' favorite shows include U.S. prime-time soap operas ("Dallas" and "Santa Barbara") and game shows. When "Dallas" was at its peak of popularity on the island, many young Tubuai women started cutting their traditionally long hair short so as to look more like Pam, a "Dallas" leading female character.

Before television reception became widely available, various community groups rented movies from Papeete and showed them at the school gymnasium to make money for their activities. Movies mainly from the United States and France were shown almost every Friday and Saturday night, and church groups, craft associations, or school groups sold admission tickets and snacks to overflow crowds.

Western Medical Care

The island's clinic, a small colonial-style building, is staffed by two French doctors and several Tahitian nurses. Until recently, islanders could just walk in and receive treatment free of charge. In the last few years, those who do not receive medical benefits through their government jobs must now register with the office of social welfare (Caisse de la Prévoyance Sociale) in order to receive medical care; it is still free of charge, however.

Although traditional Tahitian herbal medicine (*ra'au Tahiti*) and massage are practiced regularly by most island families (see Hooper 1985), they also consult the French doctor when illnesses become acute or recurrent. In addition, the government makes access to family welfare payments contingent on parents taking infants and school-age children to the clinic for regular checkups. In the case of a serious medical emergency, the doctor radios to Papeete and a medical evacuation plane (paid for by the territory) is sent to transport the patient to the territorial hospital there.

▲ A Niche in the Regional and World Economies: Market Linkages and Commodity Production

While Tubuai is now well integrated politically and administratively into the territory/French state, its integration into regional and world markets has proven to be more problematic. To promote commodity production and export from Tubuai as one part of its import substitution strategy, the government has had to create an infrastructure for production, transport, and marketing that had not previously existed.

European Vegetable Production

Government planners decided in the late 1950s that Tubuaians could be readily transformed into "successful peasant farmers" (see Thompson and Adloff 1971), producing European vegetables for Papeete markets. To promote this, the newly installed agricultural service, Service de l'Économie Rurale (SER), the government's rural development agency, gave islanders free seeds and fertilizers and arranged for the vegetables to be transported to and marketed in Papeete. Islanders responded enthusiastically to the new cash-earning opportunity, quickly adopting the new cultigens and steadily increasing output between 1960 and 1968 (SER 1960–1975). In 1968 Tubuai exported over 500 metric tons of vegetables to Papeete.

Although information from the 1960s and early 1970s is sketchy at best, lists of vegetable farmers included in the official agricultural reports of these years (SER 1960–1975) suggest that only a relatively small group of farmers specialized in vegetable cultivation; in other words, participation was not widespread (at least on any significant scale).

Despite the early successes in vegetable production, by the late 1960s problems in transporting and marketing the perishable produce were becoming increasingly intractable (SER 1960–1975). At that time, the agricultural service depended on merchant schooners to transport the vegetables, and ship captains were increasingly disgruntled over their losses due to spoilage en route. In 1971, for example, 20 percent of all carrots and cabbages were lost during transport, and islanders describe how it was common at that time to see vegetables rotting on the wharf.

Rather abruptly in the early 1970s, the SER reduced its participation in the vegetable project and told islanders to scale back their production. The annual agricultural report of 1969 expressed concern over Tubuai's "overproduction," although island output had not come close to meeting the regional demand for fresh European vegetables (SER 1969). The rapid rise and then fall of Tubuai vegetable production through the 1960s can be seen in Figure 5.1. Through the 1970s, production declined further, and by 1980 the SER was no longer exporting any green vegetables from Tubuai.

Although efficient transport and marketing were undoubtedly serious problems, events taking place in the regional economy also directly contributed to the failure of Tubuai's vegetable project (see Lockwood 1988b). In the 1960s, Chinese sharecroppers on Tahiti had started to move into the lucrative vegetable business (see Thompson and Adloff 1971). By the end of the decade they were producing a more reliable, less expensive, and fresher supply of vegetables for Papeete. Thus, one of the major rationales behind the Tubuai project, the absence of regional production and supply, had been eliminated. Morever, many Papeete merchants preferred selling canned imports from New Zealand, France, and the United States because the imports were cheaper than Tubuai produce

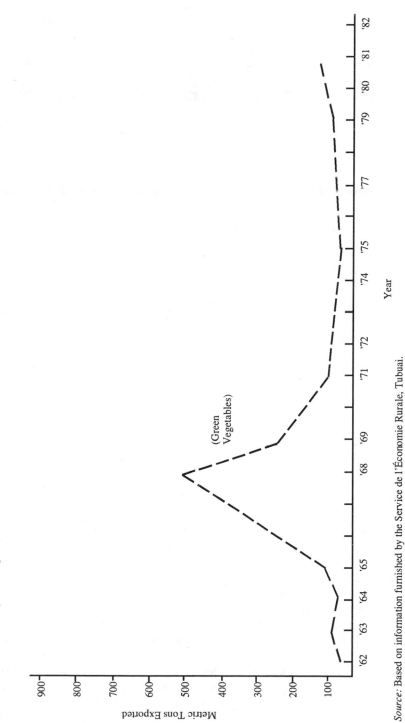

Figure 5.1 Tubuai Green Vegetable Exports, 1962–1981

Source: Based on information furnished by the Service de l'Économie Rurale, Tubuai.

(SER 1977b) and generated a higher profit margin (Thompson and Adloff 1971).

Through the 1970s, a small group of farmers continued to cultivate vegetables and to sell them locally in the island's expanding internal market (see Table 5.1). The island's schools purchased produce for student meals and the growing number of wage earners (government employees) had started to purchase, instead of producing, some of their own food. A number of island families also began to specialize at this time—mostly on a small scale—in the production and local sale of fish, fresh meats, taro, and fruits (watermelon and grapefruit) for local sales (see Table 5.1).

Table 5.1 Tubuai Commodity Sales: Local and Export

				Commodity (1,000 kgs)				
	Vegetables	Potatoes	Fish	Meat	Taro	Coffee	Copra	Fruit
Year								
1960	0.3	none	none	14.3	11.1	66.3	35.8	none
1965	70.2	none	none	36.3	25.0	27.5	1.1	none
1972	87.5	none	none	26.0	6.0	19.6	none	none
1975	45.0	49.9	25.0	16.3	6.0	22.3	16.4	none
1980	65.0	224.0	29.7	?	8.7	25.0	none	16.0
1983	180.0	545.0	29.0	14.0	16.0	30.0	none	48.0
1986	240.0	941.5	?	20.0	12.0	none	none	63.0
1990	546.8	1203.0	?	50.1	6.5	none	none	59.4

Note: Information was obtained from the annual reports of the Service de l'Économie Rurale, Tubuai.

The Potato Project

Following the demise of the project for vegetable exports, government planners reassessed Tubuai's potential contribution to the regional economy and decided that the island was best suited to the cultivation of cool-weather root crops, particularly potatoes. Long-term plans included islanders' production of carrots and onions, as well. These cool-weather crops do not grow well in the damp tropical climates of the northern islands and are not produced anywhere in the territory except in the Australs. Moreover, they are easily transported over long distances without spoilage. As with green vegetable production, the benefit to the regional economy would be import substitution and development of the rural agricultural sector.

The potato program was introduced to Tubuai farmers in the mid-1970s, although regular production did not commence until 1979. To encourage farmer participation, the project was implemented so as to minimize production uncertainties and remove barriers, such as a lack of capital, that might prevent farmers from cultivating. The SER, working in conjunction with an independent government development agency, the Société de Développement d'Agriculture et de la Pêche (SDAP), handles all aspects of production and marketing except the cultivation process itself. A farmer signs up with the SDAP to plant a certain number of kilograms of seed potatoes the coming season (three winter months). The seed potatoes are then ordered from New Zealand and Australia. At the same time, the farmer orders the fertilizers and insecticides he or she will need and signs up to rent the SDAP's tractor or bulldozer if land is to be cleared.

Until 1990, the costs of the various inputs were subsidized by the government to reduce the overall costs of production. Seed potatoes were subsidized at 30 percent and fertilizers and tractor rentals at 60 percent. Thus, in 1987, seed potatoes cost 115CFP/kg (about $1.10/kg), but farmers paid only 85CFP/kg.

When farmers sign up with the project, they automatically receive a low-interest loan (3 percent, which rose to 6 percent in 1986) from SOCREDO (Société de Crédit de l'Océanie, based in Papeete) to cover cultivation costs. At harvest, farmers are required to sell their entire crop to the SDAP (at the government-stipulated price), and part of the earnings are used to cover the incurred debt. A farmer who plants one ton (metric) of seed potatoes (about 0.4 hectare) incurs costs of about $2,300. In a good year, that farmer can earn between $1,000 and $2,000 (after costs).

The *Tuhaa Pae,* and occasionally another cargo ship, makes frequent and regular stops at Tubuai to transport the potato harvest (and other commodities) to Papeete. The SDAP arranges to sell the potatoes to stores, restaurants, and hotels, calculating the price island farmers will receive for their potatoes based on how much they can be sold for in Papeete. The SDAP is a government-affiliated, nonprofit agency, and it does not make money on the project. In 1986, Tubuai producers received 85CFP/kg[1] ($0.85/kg) for their potatoes, and the SDAP sold them to Papeete wholesalers for about 113CFP/kg ($1.13/kg). The wholesalers then sold them to markets where consumers paid 130–150CFP/kg ($1.30–$1.50/kg).

The various provisions of the project mean that virtually any individual with access to land, and that includes almost every Tubuai islander, can theoretically plant potatoes. Capital is not required to start planting, and the SDAP's cultivation machinery effectively reduces labor inputs by performing the most labor-intensive phase of production, land clearing. Family labor is usually sufficient for planting, mounding, and harvesting. Moreover, cultivation risks are reduced because farmers know that the sale and marketing of their potatoes is guaranteed. In addition, the government has at various times in the past supported the sale of Tubuai potatoes in Papeete markets by halting the importation of less expensive foreign potatoes.

Participation in the potato project and output increased steadily. By the late 1980s, over 70 percent of all Tubuai households were cultivating potatoes (264 farmers representing 204 of Tubuai's approximately 300 households).

Despite increasing levels of participation and output each year, agricultural officials recognized in the late 1980s that the project could not continue to expand indefinitely and that production levels would have to stabilize. Of the record harvest in 1987—1,800 tons—almost 200 tons spoiled when the SDAP was unable to market it. Because the potato season is a brief three months, much of Tubuai's harvest falls upon (and cannot be absorbed by) Papeete markets at the same time. Staggered planting has reduced this problem somewhat but not completely. Between 1988 and 1990, output was limited to and stabilized at about 1,200 tons. Once again, the fragility and inherent limitations of Tubuai's marketing and transport linkages had appeared, imposing constraints on island farmers and limiting their production options.

Renewed Interest in Green Vegetable Exports

Papeete merchants once again began to show interest in Tubuai green vegetables in the early 1980s (see Table 5.1). During the 1970s, the Tahiti tourist industry had expanded greatly and demand for fresh produce had increased. But Chinese sharecroppers and other Society Islands producers could not keep pace with Papeete demand during the hot, wet summer months (December through February), when production levels always declined. Because these months are significantly cooler and drier on Tubuai, it was hoped that its farmers could help meet the growing demand.

During the 1980s, a small group of Tubuai entrepreneurs began to make use of the linkages created by the government to export vegetables themselves (mainly carrots) to Papeete clients (hotels, restaurants, etc.). In addition, a French entrepreneur from Papeete came to the island in 1984 and signed up farmers to produce vegetables for him, which he then sold in Papeete. But Papeete market conditions were difficult to predict because vegetable production in the Society Islands was highly variable. By 1986, the French entrepreneur had literally disappeared while still owing islanders for their last shipments of produce. By the late 1980s, only one Tubuai entrepreneur remained active (and only marginally so) in highly risky vegetable exports.

In 1989 and 1990, Tubuai's government-sponsored agricultural cooperative also began playing a role in green vegetable exports, attempting to aid farmers by arranging transport and marketing for their vegetables. Although 1990 was a successful year—over 576 tons of green vegetables were exported—the co-op also ran into significant marketing difficulties. Consequently, in 1991 it decided to cut back production—a move now

Goods from Papeete being unloaded from the Tuhaa Pae, *the cargo ship that visits Tubuai regularly* (photo: Lockwood)

The central, open-air market in Papeete where some of Tubuai's exported produce is sold (photo: Lockwood)

very familiar to Tubuai farmers. This decision both frustrated and discouraged island farmers, and the future of Tubuai green vegetable exports once again looked bleak.

A Roller Coaster Ride for Island Farmers

The fortunes of the few island families who steadfastly chose to specialize in vegetable cultivation through the 1970s and 1980s reflected the roller coaster–like ups and downs of the development project itself. In 1980, when I first met the Tarohe family—Taputu, Marie, and their five children—they were vegetable farmers who could not make a living from the meager quantities of produce they were able to sell to the local high school. During the 1970s, Taputu had been one the island's largest vegetable producers, but by 1980 the agricultural service was no longer exporting and he had fallen back on the limited local market.

The couple's major source of income had become craft production. Taputu was among a small number of local men who carved wooden sculptures and replicas of ancient Tahitian bowls, spears, and lances and other artifacts. He sold a small number of these to the island's French residents (schoolteachers and administrators) and to occasional visitors to the island. Marie sewed Tahitian quilts (*tifaifai*) and plaited pandanus mats and hats for sale. Both belonged to the government-subsidized craft association located in the island district where they lived.

The family's earnings from crafts and vegetables were supplemented by the occasional slaughter of a pig and sale of pork to other families, by the small-scale, seasonal gathering and sale of coffee beans from their ancient familial plantations in the mountains, and by family allocations (about $100 a month). Altogether, the Tarohes earned about $550 a month in 1980.

Most of their income went to buy household necessities and clothing and to maintain the old truck that Taputu managed to keep running. Avoiding purchases of expensive canned and imported foods at the store, they produced almost all of their own food from their taro and vegetable gardens, and Taputu fished regularly with his sons. Like many island men, Taputu had carved his own outrigger canoe from the trunk of a large tree. A decision to allow another family to *fa'a'amu* (informally adopt) their sixth child, born in 1979, was explained by Marie as related to the difficulties of supporting another child.

In 1980, Taputu was one of the first island farmers to sign up to plant in the new potato project. That year the family cultivated two tons of seed potatoes and harvested six tons of potatoes, earning about $1,800 after expenses. They continued planting each year thereafter, and potato earnings were increasingly becoming an important income supplement for them.

When I returned to Tubuai in 1985, the transformation in the family's previously demoralized situation was astounding. Taputu had joined ranks with the French entrepreneur (described previously) who had come to the island looking for vegetables to export to Papeete. Taputu not only served as this man's local agent, but also he was one of his major producers. In 1984, the Tarohes produced over forty-five tons of vegetables (mostly cabbages and tomatoes).[2] With their earnings—about $30,000—Taputu purchased a new Peugeot truck and set aside money to refurbish their old run-down house.

Having moved once again into vegetable cultivation on a large scale, almost all of the Tarohes' other economic activities, except potato cultivation, came to a halt. They gave up producing crafts altogether and abandoned their taro gardens to the weeds. Store-bought rice replaced taro as the family's staple.

Taputu continued to work with the French entrepreneur until the latter's sudden disappearance. He then shifted to a local Tubuai entrepreneur who had established marketing contacts with a number of Papeete hotels through his Chinese merchant daughter-in-law who lived in the city. In 1986, another good year, the Tarohes produced and sold seventy-one tons of green vegetables. In 1987, Taputu also harvested the island's record potato crop of the year (forty-five tons).

Taputu attributed his great success with green vegetables and potatoes to his careful tending of his fields. Moreover, he did not "economize" (islanders' own word) on fertilizers and insecticides to save money like most farmers. But Taputu was also different from many other farmers in his disregard of the phases of the moon for planting and harvesting. Although he believed that taro and other local crops should be planted by the moon, he had personally concluded that for vegetables, "there was no moon."

By 1987, the Tarohes had enlarged and refurbished their house with a new Western-style kitchen, glass windows, furniture, and a television set. Taputu had purchased a second new Peugeot truck. The Tarohes, now earning over $45,000 a year, had moved well up into the highest income bracket on the island.

Although the family kept largely to themselves and were involved in relatively few community activities (they were one of the few families who never attended church), Marie believes that their spectacular and relatively rapid affluence caused other islanders to ostracize them increasingly. She believes that others were jealous and purposefully sent their dogs into the vegetables to trample the young plants. Such jealousy frequently results in accusations of sorcery, although neither Marie nor Taputu believed that sorcery had been directed at them.

When I returned to the island in 1991, I found that the family's fortunes had once again reversed for the worse. Taputu had almost stopped cultivating green vegetables, leaving his fields fallow during all but the three winter months when he still planted potatoes. The Tubuai entrepreneur who had marketed his vegetables in Papeete had also run into problems, and sometimes Taputu would have to wait six to eight months to get paid. He was able to sell only nine tons of carrots in 1990, and 1991 looked dismal.

To make up for some of the large loss in income, Taputu and Marie returned to their taro gardens and began producing and selling *popoi,* a traditional Tahitian specialty of mashed and fermented taro wrapped in banana leaves. One large packet sells for 500CFP, or about $5.00. Each week they left twenty to thirty packets with a neighbor to sell to passersby at her roadside stand. They were able to earn about $400–$500 a month in this way. As Marie explained, selling the *popoi* was certain, whereas vegetables were not.

Other Export Commodities: Coffee and Crafts

In addition to green vegetables and potatoes, the government also supports and subsidizes the production of other kinds of commodities, including coffee and crafts. Both have experienced only marginal success.

Crafts. To encourage the production and marketing of crafts—pandanus mats and hats, wooden replicas of ancient artifacts, shell necklaces, and *tifaifai*—the government created Artisan associations and offered them various kinds of financial aid. Because women are the producers of most crafts (all except wooden artifacts), this is one development effort geared toward women.

A Rurutu woman and some of the hats she has made to sell (photo: Lockwood)

In the early 1980s, one crafts association on Tubuai received a $7,000 government grant, which it used to build a *fare ni'au,* a traditional-style, thatched-roof house, in which to display and sell its products, and to purchase several sewing machines, a small electric generator, and some power woodworking tools. Various agencies in Papeete also help the groups to market their crafts to tourists and others there.

Throughout the 1980s, the production and sale of crafts has increased substantially in the territory. Nevertheless, the limited market demand for these items has meant that they remain an insignificant source of income on most islands, including Tubuai. The nearby island of Rurutu is a major exception; Rurutu women are known throughout the territory for their beautiful *tifaifai* and finely plaited mats and hats, and many send their items to Papeete to be sold.

Coffee. Coffee was first planted in the interior mountainous zones of several of the Austral Islands, including Tubuai, during the early 1900s. Islanders gathered the ripe coffee beans, removed the pulp by hand, dried the beans in the sun, and then sold them to the local Chinese merchant families, who exported them to Papeete. Although Tubuai exported sixty-six tons of coffee in 1960, production fell off heavily after that (see Table 5.1). Coffee production was labor intensive and the earnings were meager. As a result, the mountain plantations were increasingly ignored as new economic

A teenage girl laying her family's recently gathered coffee beans in the sun to dry (photo: Lockwood)

opportunities became available in the early 1960s, although islanders did export about twenty to twenty-five tons each year. Having adopted the French custom of breakfasting on coffee with milk and French bread, most Tubuai families simply gathered small quantities of cherry coffee for their own home consumption.

To promote coffee production and export in the Australs, the government built a small coffee-processing plant on Tubuai in the early 1980s. Tubuai and the other nearby Austral Islands could have their coffee processed, packaged, and exported to Papeete. But most important, to interest islanders in coffee production, the government raised (and subsidized) the price to coffee producers to 390CFP/kg (about $3.90/kg). Subsequently, production and replanting of plantations increased rapidly. Unfortunately, a coffee rust disease struck the islands in the mid-1980s, causing the trees to produce little. By 1991, the plantations were again producing, and coffee may become a major export crop of the 1990s.

▲ Consumerism and the Flow of Imports

The revenues that flow to the island in the form of government salaries, subsidies, and welfare payments, as well as income from government-subsidized commodity production, quickly flow back out again as islanders

Chinese proprietors of one of the island's two general stores (photo: Lance Rasbridge)

use the money to purchase an impressive (by Western standards) array of imported goods in the international marketplace. With the exception of staple foods (mainly taro) and some craft items, islanders no longer produce any of their own tools or equipment (except canoes), clothing, or household items. Tubuai's two general stores stock canned foods and household/manufactured items ordered from wholesale distributors in Papeete, who themselves order from Australia, New Zealand, France, Japan, and the United States. On Tubuai, one can purchase Heineken beer, fresh lamb from New Zealand, a selection of French cheeses and wines, Japanese rice, Campbell's soup, and Pampers disposable diapers (among other things).

After electricity was installed in the mid-1980s, islanders rushed to purchase imported manufactured items and appliances, including washing machines, refrigerators and freezers, television sets, and even videocassette recorders (one of the Chinese stores now rents movies on cassette at $10 a day). The bigger items are purchased in Papeete and transported on the cargo ship to Tubuai. The massive surge in islanders' consumption that took place in the 1980s—exemplified by the case of Taputu and Marie—can be seen in Table 5.2.

Table 5.2 Number of Households That Owned Major Consumer Items, 1981 and 1987[a]

	1981	1987
Item		
Motor vehicle	55	102
Television	9	177
Freezer	45	182
Washing machine	[3][b]	128
Boat motor	(unknown)	85
Videocassette recorder	[3]	63
Telephone	[3]	89
Electricity, in 1981 by generator	25	204

[a]In 1981, there were approximately 200–210 Tubuai households; in 1987, there were approximately 300.

[b]Number in brackets is estimated; in 1981, these items were owned only by the top-level government officials on the island.

Islanders' consumerism is directly promoted by (and some might say actually created by) the effectively aggressive marketing and distribution activities of transnational corporations throughout the Pacific. Such marketing motivates islanders to purchase the latest-model Japanese vehicles and state-of-the-art German, U.S., and Japanese electronics and appliances, and made these items actually available (through Papeete) on this remote island of about 2,000 farmers and fishermen in the middle of the South Pacific Ocean.

The sight of a television antenna perched atop a *fare ni'au* is a potent symbol of one of the major ways Tubuai participates in international capitalism. Producing virtually no manufactured goods itself, the French territory—and islanders' present lifestyle—is staggeringly dependent on imports from the industrialized nations.

▲ Church Networks

One of the most powerful linkages that connect Tubuai islanders to other island societies in the territory and to international populations around the world is shared church affiliations. Islanders belong to a number of different Christian denominations, including the Evangelical Church of French Polynesia, or "Protestants" (37 percent of all families); the Catholic church (12 percent); the Church of Jesus Christ of Latter-Day Saints, or Mormons (29 percent); the Reorganized Church of Jesus Christ of Latter-Day Saints, or "Sanitos" (14 percent); and the Seventh-Day Adventists (6 percent).

Most Tahitians throughout the territory today are Protestants, the legacy of their ancestors' conversion by the London Missionary Society (LMS). LMS missionaries first settled on Tubuai in 1822 (Cook 1976). But missionaries representing other denominations arrived soon after and were able to convert some families to their own particular faiths.

Tubuai churches operate as branches of larger church organizations based in Papeete, and in the case of the Mormons and Sanitos, of church organizations headquartered in the United States. In the early 1980s, the heads of both the Mormon and Sanito church organizations in Papeete were Americans. The small Catholic church on the island is overseen by a French priest.

Church conferences are regularly held in Papeete and many Tubuaians attend. Camps for church youth groups are also regularly held either in Papeete or on various centrally located islands. Just in the last several years, members of the Sanito and Mormon churches have traveled to the United States to participate in major international church functions.

In addition to organizing church conferences, parent church organizations send pastors and teachers to the outer islands and generally provide a regional (or international) operating structure for local churches. The Mormon church is one of the most active in this regard. The American Mormon church sends missionaries to Tubuai for two-year stints; in 1980–1981, the missionaries were an elderly couple from Arizona, and in 1987 there were two young American men serving on the island. In addition, the International Mormon church financed the building of a modern church building and basketball court for Tubuai's Mahu district in the mid-1980s.

The Christian church is an extremely important part of islanders' lives, and with few exceptions Tubuaians are devout and faithful churchgoers. Most Tubuaians attend a church service, meeting, or function at least two or three times a week. Church activities include not only Sunday services, but also regular evening prayer meetings, youth groups and sport groups, women's church groups, and various community events aimed at fundraising (dances, food sales, and so on). Most island families make regular financial contributions to their church (tithing), money that is ultimately channeled to the church's parent organization either in Papeete, France, or the United States.

Thus, through its religious affiliations, Tubuai's tiny population is actively linked into worldwide church organizations, many of which extend islanders' contacts to nations other than France. These linkages involve not only social, educational, and cultural exchanges, but also flows of financial resources. The American Mormon church is one sect that has clearly invested in its Tubuai congregation; it is also the fastest-growing denomination on the island.

▲ Intraregional Migration

Today, the constant movement of people between Tubuai and Papeete creates one of the most important linkages between Tubuai and the region as a whole. Frequent intra-island mobility is made possible by regular air flights (Air Tahiti) and sea (shipping) connections. Most of this movement can be characterized as of the circulating type, in which rural populations maintain frequent contacts with the city to gain access to resources absent in the rural area (see Graves and Graves 1974; Spoehr 1969). These resources include schools, health care, church conferences, legal services, political patronage, and consumer goods.

But it was the economic boom of the 1960s and the availability of wage work associated with the building of the nuclear installations (CEP) that brought a literal flood of rural migrants from the outer islands to the city. Unlike most visitors to the city, these migrants intended to leave their economically stagnant, more traditional home islands permanently.

Such population movements between less developed rural areas and urban industrial centers are a major structural feature of the capitalist world system. In the international division of labor, migrants from less developed regions form a pool of relatively unskilled, low-paid labor for capitalist enterprises during periods of expansion. In many cases, these migrants send part of their wages (remittances) home to help support family members.

Throughout the 1960s and early 1970s, rural Tahitian migrants in

Papeete formed such a pool of unskilled, low-paid labor. Some Tahitians had also migrated to New Caledonia to work in the expanding French nickel industry there. Although little information is available on their remitting patterns, it appears that unlike many other Pacific migrant populations, Tahitians sent few remittances home (see Lockwood 1990). In general, it appears that Tahitians did not (and do not) maintain strong networks (linkages) with kin who have migrated.

By the end of the decade and completion of the CEP, however, this pool of rural migrant labor in Papeete had became superfluous. Through the ensuing economic recession of the 1970s and into the early 1980s, unemployment, poverty, and overcrowding contributed to mounting social unrest in Papeete. It was at this point that the government stepped in, as one part of its regional development efforts, to create specific linkages that would reverse population flows and return these migrants to their home islands.

The government's creation of new economic opportunities on Tubuai attracted many of the previous migrants who were finding it increasingly hard to make a living in Papeete. By the 1980s, it had become one of the most expensive cities in the world. These migrants believed that they could return to Tubuai and probably find a job or become involved in commercial agriculture, and that their standard of living might actually improve. Within the Tahitian familial land tenure system (see Chapter 6), these migrants still retained their rights to land on Tubuai—an enduring and powerful linkage between themselves and their home island. To facilitate return migration, the government also provided various key financial aids to families. These resources helped return migrants pay for transportation and set up housing on their home islands (Connell 1985).

Between 1981 and 1987 alone, thirty-six families who had set up "permanent" residence in either Papeete or Noumea elected to return to live on Tubuai. The rapid growth in the island's population after two decades of stagnation can be seen in Table 5.3. By the late 1980s, 11 percent of all island households were composed of recent return migrants, and it appeared that rates of return were increasing. At present, French Polynesia is the only region of island Oceania where urban to rural return migration has been documented.

▲ Linkages and Dependency

Many scholars working from a world systems perspective suggest that the Western industrialized nations have created linkages (either during the colonial or modern eras) to less developed regions in order to exploit their natural resources or relatively cheap labor resources (see Wallerstein 1974; Nash 1981). The flow of resources between the core industrial nations and the periphery is never of equal value, and the West enriches itself at the

Table 5.3 Tubuai Population

Year	Population Size	Source
1775	inhabited	(Aitken 1930)
1821	900	(Aitken 1930)
1849	180	(Aitken 1930)
1892	429	(Aitken 1930)
1922	755	(Aitken 1930)
1956	1,116	(Cook 1976)
1971	1,421	(INSEE 1973)
1977	1,419	(Connell 1985)
1983	1,741	(Connell 1985)
1988	2,022	(ITSTAT 1988)

expense of peripheral regions in the system. By holding the upper hand in the international division of labor, the industrialized nations are able to dictate not only the types of resources that flow between themselves and developing regions, but also the terms of trade. Developing regions are dependent on the industrial nations to purchase their typically few primary commodities and to provide access to their industrial and manufactured goods.

But this well-known model of Third World exploitation and dependency is largely inapplicable to the situation in French Polynesia. As the discussion of the various linkages between the Tahitian islands, France, and the world system has shown, welfare state colonialism involves a reverse flow of resources: more financial and other kinds of resources flow from France to the islands than vice versa. It would be hard to say that the relatively affluent Tahitian population is economically exploited.[3] But a critical resource does flow from the islands to France, and it is one that France apparently values quite highly: Tahitian political clientage—their agreement to serve as a neocolonial satellite of France and to "rent" the islands to France for nuclear testing activities. Thus, the element of political domination is certainly present in the French Polynesian case.

The element of economic dependency is also clearly present. In 75 percent of all Tubuai households, government salaries or transfer payments are the major source of income (see Table 5.4). It is this money that generates island families' high standard of living. In only 25 percent of all Tubuai households is primary production (agriculture, fishing, crafts, and so on) the major source of income. But even most primary production, specifically the production of export-oriented commodities (green vegetables, potatoes, coffee, crafts), is government subsidized. For many reasons, including transport and marketing inefficiencies and an inability to compete with less expensive foreign imports, islanders would probably be unable to sustain commodity production without these subsidies. Thus, both the islanders who receive their income directly from the government in the

Table 5.4 Major Source of Tubuai Household Income, 1987

Source of Income	Number of Households	% of all Households
Government sector (75%)		
Employment	137	49
Pensions	58	21
Family allocations	14	5
Subtotal	209	75
Private sector (25%)		
Fish sales	21	8
Potato sales	19	7
Craft sales	4	1
Vegetable sales	15	5
Sales of indigenous crops (taro, etc.)	3	1
Small commerce (roadside stands, etc.)	4	1
Sales of fresh meats (beef and pork)	3	1
Vegetable exports	2	1
Subtotal	71	25
Total	280	100

form of salaries or pensions and those who receive it indirectly through agricultural or other subsidies are heavily dependent on French transfer payments.

With the exception of the linkages created by regional and international church networks, Tubuai's linkages to the world system have been government created and they are dependency inducing. They are also clearly artificial. The French government has effectively created an artificial political entity, an overseas territory of France, made up of five different island groups. It is also working to create an economic role for Tubuai in the regional capitalist economy and a role for French Polynesia in the world capitalist economy. The difficulties involved in sustaining these development efforts suggest just how peripheral the islands are to the world economy as it is presently constituted.

▲ Notes

1. Throughout the decade of the 1980s, the French Polynesian franc (CFP) varied in value between 75 and 120 francs per U.S. dollar. Throughout the text, I have adopted an average of 100CFP as equivalent to one U.S. dollar.
2. In the mid-1980s, Tubuai producers sold their vegetables locally and for

export at the following average prices: tomatoes (120CFP/kg); carrots (100CFP/kg); cabbage (199CFP/kg); cucumbers (80CFP/kg); green peppers (130CFP/kg).

3. One can certainly argue that rural Tahitians are exploited by capitalism, according to the standard Marxist definition of exploitation. Australian firms, for example, make a large profit by selling seed potatoes to islanders for the inflated price of $1.25/kg; they cost only about $0.10/kg in Australia, and shipping charges do not make up the difference. Transnational corporations also make substantial profits when they sell expensive manufactured goods to islanders at inflated prices. Another example: Islanders are paid about $0.85/kg for their potatoes, but retailers in Papeete sell them to consumers for between $1.50 and $2.00/kg, keeping a substantial profit for themselves. But even though capitalists siphon off Tubuai capital in these and other ways, so much money flows back to islanders through welfare state colonialism that their "exploitation" is for the most part canceled out. Islanders' high incomes and Western-style standard of living attest to that.

▲ 6

Contemporary Tubuai Socioeconomic Organization: Households, the Peasant Mode of Production, and Class

Despite rural Tahitians' extensive involvement in international capitalism—both as producers of export commodities and as consumers of imported manufactured goods—socioeconomic organization on the outer islands is best described as only "part capitalist." As in many other peripheral communities of the Third World (see Amin 1976), the local-level "capitalist transformation" many scholars thought would accompany integration into capitalist markets and "modernization" has simply not materialized.

In these communities, the penetration of capitalist relations of production has been "incomplete." The major indicator of that incompleteness is the domination of peripheral rural economies by a "peasant mode of production" (or by "commodity-producing peasant households") (see Cook 1982; Gibbon and Neocosmos 1985; Smith 1984). In this mode of production, the peasant household operates at times as a capitalist enterprise, while at others it follows precapitalist patterns.

The peasant mode of production integrates subsistence production with market-oriented production and/or wage labor. The peasant household owns its own means of production, usually land, and also provides all (or most) of its own labor; thus, it fulfills both the functions of capital and labor. Although the household is integrated into a market system and may produce commodities for that system, land and the other means of production are usually not the private property of household members. Instead, they continue to be "owned" jointly by kin or other groups. Household units possess use but not ownership rights to land, and there is no market in land (it is not a commodity).

Instead of accumulating wealth and reinvesting it in production (like good capitalists), peasant households may distribute their wealth to others—or consume it conspicuously—to gain social or religious prestige. When in need of extra labor, peasant households may participate in various kinds of cooperative or reciprocal work groups (based on kin or village ties). A market in labor is either nonexistent or undeveloped.

Although it was once thought that this so-called mixed organization was a transitional stage between precapitalist and fully capitalist relations of production, it now appears that it is a highly stable and well-integrated socioeconomic form in many parts of the less developed world. In this chapter, I describe the peasant mode of production as it is manifested on Tubuai and throughout rural Tahitian society. This includes a discussion of contemporary household socioeconomic organization, focusing on resource bases, productive activities, and social relations of production.

▲ Tubuai Households and the Organization of Production

Tubuai households are scattered around the island, a settlement pattern that reflects the centuries-old connections of island families to particular parcels of land. It has been only in the last twenty years that a town center of sorts has come into being on the island. This town center, called Mataura after the district in which it is located, is where the island's various government buildings (mayor's office, post office, and so on) and commerce (two general stores) are concentrated, opposite what used to be the island's only wharf. The main Protestant church, the clinic, and the main primary school are also located here.

Islanders usually build their houses by the road that follows the coastline around the entire island. In the 1940s and 1950s, this road was little more than a path used by islanders on horseback and on foot. As bicycles and motor vehicles became more common in the 1960s, this path was enlarged and covered over with coral gravel dredged from the lagoon. In the late 1980s, about half of it had been paved with asphalt.

Living near the road allows islanders ready access to town and to jobs, and it also means that they will be conveniently located near the coastal area and lagoon for fishing. Tubuai families typically tie their outrigger canoes to trees on the beach opposite their houses. A few families, however, live in the interior of the island. They use the island's only other road, a rough dirt road that bisects the island between the two major central-island peaks.

Traveling along the main road around the island, one passes either individual houses or clusters of houses separated by long distances of brush, trees, stands of pandanus, coconut plantations, and potato fields. Most houses today are built in a Western style (wood frame and stucco), although families also occasionally construct traditional-style *fare ni'au* out of woven pandanus and bamboo (with a coconut frond roof). The *fare ni'au* are usually temporary housing, which young couples or families use for several months to several years until they accumulate enough money or other resources to build a permanent Western-style house.

Each house is surrounded by an abundance of banana, papaya, and coconut trees, and gardens of beautiful flowers that are tended with great care by island women. At the back of the house, chickens forage freely, while a pig or cow may be tethered to a tree in an open area. Families cultivate vegetable gardens, usually near their houses, while taro is planted farther inland in the island's low-lying swampy zones or along the numerous streams that run from the central mountains to the coast.

Each household is an independent economic unit—well situated geographically to pursue a range of agricultural activities as well as fishing. Indeed, the economic activities of Tubuai households—like those of households in many peasant communities—are highly diversified. Most participate simultaneously in a number of different cash-earning options (and/or wage employment). While about half of all households include an employed member, about 80 percent are involved in the production and sale of one or more commodities. Most families (of all types) also produce much of their own food by gardening and fishing.

Tubuai households' major economic occupations and income levels are presented in Table 6.1. Low-income households (16 percent of all households) tend to be predominantly subsistence-oriented, meaning they do not include an employed member nor do they produce and sell more than a minimal quantity of household products (coded L). Low/middle income households (20 percent of all households) are usually headed by elderly couples who receive government pensions as their major source of income (coded L/M).

Middle-income households (35 percent of all households) are of two types: (1) those that market substantial quantities of their products (coded M1), or (2) those in which the household head is employed (unskilled) (coded M2). High-income households (28 percent of all households) are of several types: (1) those in which a member holds a skilled job (coded H0), (2) those in which both male and female household heads are employed (coded H1), (3) those in which the household head is employed and the household is also a significant market producer (coded H2), or (4) those in which household members are large-scale market producers or exporters (coded H3).

Households and Kinship

On Tubuai, most households are composed of nuclear families (75 percent of all households), and young couples aspire to build their own house for themselves and their children as soon as possible on family lands. This may not be possible at first, and young couples typically live with one set of parents for several years until they are financially able to make their own way. There appears to be no preference for virilocal or uxorilocal residence; circumstances usually dictate the choice. Thus, some Tubuai households are extended in this manner ("composite," about 12 percent), while others sometimes include an elderly grandparent, aunt, or cousin. Approximately 25

Table 6.1 Tubuai Households (HH): Incomes and Occupations, 1987[a]

Socioeconomic Status (Income[b]/Occupation)	Number of HHs	% of all HHs	Share of Total Island Income (%)[c]
Low income	46	16	4
$2,000–$4,500			
(L) Subsistence			
Low/middle income	58	20	12
$3,000–$4500			
(L/M) Pension			
Middle income			31
$4,500–$16,000			
(M1) Markets	27	10	
(M2) Employed	72	25	
High income			53
$16,000–$35,000			
(H0) Skilled employment	35	12	
(H1) Dual employment	24	8	
(H2) Markets/employment	13	5	
(H3) Major marketer	9	3	
Total	284	99	100

[a]These figures on household income were compiled from household census data and budgets and from information furnished by employers and local government agencies. There may be as much as a 5 percent error in the mean.

[b]All figures are in U.S. dollars ($). In 1981, one U.S. dollar was equivalent to 75 Communautés Françaises du Pacifique (CFP) francs; in 1987, 100 CFP francs equaled $1.00.

[c]Calculations were made by multiplying the mean annual income (left-hand column) by the number of households in that category, and then dividing by the total number of households.

percent of all Tubuai households are composed of extended families of various types. The average Tubuai household has five members; 71 percent of all households on the island have six or fewer members, while 21 percent have seven to nine members and 9 percent have ten to fifteen members.

Some families also include children who have been informally adopted (*fa'a' amu*), a common Tahitian practice; about 25 percent of all Tubuai families have either given or received a child in this way (Panoff 1970). Most often parents adopt a grandchild—the offspring of an unmarried son or daughter. There may be other reasons for *fa'a' amu*, however, such as economic hardship (the Tarohe family situation) or death of a parent.

Tubuaians consider all of their mother's relatives and all of their father's relatives to be their relatives (*feti'i*), or bilateral kindred. This group, however, does not constitute a corporate group in any sense, nor does it play any significant role in island social life. For the most part, one's kin are expected to offer support or aid when needed, although islanders expect such aid to be strictly reciprocated. Other than for whatever mutual aid might be offered, one's *feti'i* are significant only regarding familial land ownership.

Contemporary Land Ownership and Use

About 80 percent of all land on Tubuai is owned jointly by groups of kin, while the rest is owned by individuals or by the territorial government (see Joralemon 1983; Ravault 1979). Every islander, male or female, has inherited land rights from his or her mother and father, who inherited them from his or her mother or father. Because families typically own a number of different parcels, each contemporary islander has land rights to various parcels dispersed in different parts of the island.

As noted earlier, the present land system reflects repeated efforts on the part of French colonial officials to create a system of individual land ownership. Their meddling in the land system effectively transformed the indigenous system into one of bilateral inheritance. But islanders continued to pass their land on to their offspring as one large undifferentiated group, ignoring the notion of individual titles. Until islanders began to use land for cash-cropping, at which time the land became increasingly "scarce" and family disputes increased, there was little rationale for islanders to alter their land use/ownership patterns.

In the present system, if there are ten co-owners of one parcel of *fenua feti'i* (family land), then each co-owner technically owns one-tenth of it (which one-tenth is not specified). In most cases, however, many of those ten co-owners no longer reside on the island (due to emigration) and/or are not active cultivators. If there are two resident cultivators on the island, then each will effectively have use access to one-half of the parcel. But, it is also possible that other co-owners may have granted their use rights to some other individual (usually also kin).

Those co-owners who are resident on the island and who wish to cultivate the land will agree among themselves as to how to divide it. In some cases, a family head, frequently a grandparent, is asked to coordinate use or to give permission for family members to cultivate certain areas. When families cannot arrange matters among themselves, which occurs only rarely because of the relative abundance of land, a case may be taken before the French *gendarmes*. They mediate until legal procedures for permission or division are agreed upon by the family.

It is important to note that according to Tahitian principles, ownership of the land itself is a separate matter from the ownership of improvements (gardens, plantations) on the land. Although a group of kin may own a piece of land, gardens and other improvements and their products belong to the individual who created (planted) them. Thus, actual patterns of land use on Tubuai are highly individualized. The only exception to this is long-standing tree crop plantations (coconuts and coffee). Although originally owned by the person who planted them, these plantations are usually inherited by that person's heirs as a group. Thus, like land, tree crop plantations typically have numerous co-owners, although they are not necessarily the same group of people who are joint co-owners of the land.

It is also important to note that in actual practice, the rights of male and female inheritors to own and use land are truly equivalent. According to both the French legal system and islanders' worldview, males and females are not distinguished in any way regarding land. In commenting on the future inheritance of his or her land (actually co-ownership rights in parcels), for example, an elderly grandmother or grandfather will state quite clearly that grandsons and granddaughters have the same needs for land and should receive equal portions. This is true regardless of the fact that men are considered to be the farmers. Because postmarital residence is just as likely to be on the familial land of the bride as of the groom, a daughter (or granddaughter) and her future family may well use her land to earn their living. It never enters an islander's mind that sons but not daughters should be given land, or that daughters should be given land but that it should actually be controlled by male family members.

Thus, by virtue of their kinship ties, every islander "owns" land, possessing joint use and ownership rights to parcels with others. But there are land-rich and land-poor families. Particular situations depend mostly on familial demographics over time. Individuals who technically own very little land can "borrow" it from land-rich kin or neighbors and thus have effective use of extensive lands; this happens frequently. Access to land in many cases is determined by whether or not particular families have activated all of the possible kin networks to borrow land (temporarily) from others. Such borrowing may be from the relatives of either the male or female household head.

While it is possible to determine how much land is actually cultivated by particular Tubuai households, it is extremely difficult to determine how much they actually "own" or have access to through various kin ties (which may or may not be activated). The average family intensively cultivates usually less than one hectare (2.2 acres), and probably closer to half a hectare of land (or 5,000 square meters); this includes land planted in taro, green vegetables, and potatoes. Vegetables may be planted in the same field reserved for potatoes during the three-month winter potato season. Most families also tend one or two hectares of tree crops, although these may be located on parcels of land apart from their house and gardens.

The spread of commercial agriculture, particularly potato cultivation, has made well-draining agricultural lands on this generally swampy island more scarce. In a household survey in 1981, 63 percent of all island families said they had enough agricultural land to meet their needs, while 37 percent said they did not. By the late 1980s, a similar survey showed that only 51 percent of all families said they had sufficient land; this includes all kinds of land—*fenua feti'i,* individually owned parcels, and land borrowed from kin. While commercial agriculture is placing increasing demands on available land, it is clear that the majority of all Tubuai families still have sufficient land to meet their needs.

It has only been in recent years that islanders have considered individualizing their holdings by going through the cumbersome and expensive French legal process of dividing parcels among all of the legitimate co-owners (many of whom have long ago emigrated from the island). While desires to individualize are in part linked to the rapid spread of commercial agriculture, they are also linked to a growing number of familial disputes over land. Most of these disputes have to do with young couples' plans to build new, modern houses on their family lands—a sizable investment. In these cases, all co-owners must give their permission for the construction because, at least in theory, the house will remain there permanently and no other use may be made of that area of land. It is not necessary to obtain permission to build a traditional-style *fare ni'au*, a construction that is considered temporary. Sometimes kin do not agree to allow a family member to build a permanent house, knowing that such permanent construction will preclude their own future use of the land for either agriculture or a housesite.

Surprisingly, it is the largest commercial farmers who particularly want to maintain familial ownership. Under this system, they may plant the familial lands of absent kin, and usually after receiving permission from only one or two relatives living on the island. This enables them to cultivate large areas of land that technically do not belong to them. Other family members (the actual owners) agree to this because they benefit from the farmer having cleared the land, and they know they can reclaim rights to it at any time. If land were divided and sections of parcels were legally owned by individual family members, large-scale farmers would no longer have such open access to the lands they freely use now. If land were private property, it is likely that owners would ask farmers to pay rent to use it.

Despite a slight increase in legal land divisions, there is virtually no market for land on Tubuai. A few parcels have been sold, although most of these were purchased by the government for the construction of schools, the post office, and other public buildings. In the few cases where legal land divisions have taken place, family members did not do so planning to then sell their portions. Instead, they wanted to have their "part," mostly so that they could construct new, permanent houses.

Familial attachment to land remains strong on Tubuai today despite the many changes that have taken place in recent decades. Even young people criticize elders who have sold land to the government in the past, thereby depriving them of parcels they could farm or use for housesites today. Most important, the present land system appears to be highly compatible with the Tubuai organization of production and with the household-level scale of enterprise intrinsic to the Tahitian commodity-producing peasant household.

The Organization of Labor

The vast majority of all Tubuai families provide all of their own labor for their various productive activities. On occasion they will work cooperatively in groups (*pupu*), although labor sharing is strictly reciprocal. These groups are typically made up of kin or members of the same church. Only a small group of large-scale cultivators of vegetables and potatoes (about 9 percent of all families), hire workers at peak labor times.

Within the household unit itself, tasks are differentially assigned by age and gender, and the contemporary division of labor is much like the one described for the early 1900s (see Chapter 3). Generally, women maintain the household, care for children, sew and wash clothing (all by hand until recently), and process and prepare food. Much of a woman's day is taken up with her *ménage,* or housework. Women also occasionally fish on the reef and perform many secondary tasks in fields and gardens (e.g., plant seedlings, weed, and so on). Women are also now cultivating their own independent potato fields, and some produce craft items for sale.

Tubuai men fish and perform the majority of all agricultural labor. The arduous turning of the heavy, swampy soil in preparation to plant taro, as well as lagoon fishing, are considered to be male tasks and inappropriate for women. There are exceptions, however, and on occasion women do perform these tasks. Men also construct canoes and houses and tend horses, pigs, and cows. They do most of the cooking on special feasting occasions and when the *umu,* earth oven, is prepared (usually also only on special occasions).

When men are employed and thus somewhat removed from direct participation in agriculture and fishing, their wives do not take over these tasks. If a teenaged son is not available, the family will purchase more of its food at the store and from other families (usually nonemployed commodity producers). Although time allocation data on the hours spent working (at the household) by men and women are not available, I would guess that women simply do not have enough hours in the day to assume men's tasks in addition to their own.

Children perform many small tasks around the household, and young girls are particularly expected to watch over smaller children. Because children are in school most of the day, their overall labor contributions are minimal, except for weekends during the potato season when one can see whole families working out in the fields. Teenage daughters who are no longer attending school take over a significant portion of the housework, freeing their mothers to spend more hours in craft production or church activities, or to cultivate potatoes if they choose.

On occasion, members of different households get together to form a *pupu,* or cooperative work group, when a particularly large or tedious task must be completed. The group meets at an assigned time each day, usually for a specified period of time (several hours), and rotates its labor among its members. The most common type of *pupu* is a women's group formed to

weave large pandanus floor mats or other items. However, women sometimes form *pupus* to work cooperatively in each other's potato fields. Young
men, usually cousins, occasionally form *pupus* to prepare their families' taro
patches.

A few families who are large-scale cultivators hire other islanders to
work for them during labor-intensive periods. This includes potato planting
and harvesting and the harvesting and washing of carrots for market.
Tubuaians say that it is hard to find workers because everyone wants to work
for themselves. Nevertheless, between the early and late 1980s, the number
of individuals who worked as paid agricultural laborers doubled from about
twenty to forty persons, an increase related to the rapid expansion of potato
cultivation. The average worker earns about $35 a day, including meals.

It is surprising that the vast majority of these paid agricultural workers
on Tubuai are women, especially since men perform most agricultural labor.
When one remembers, however, that women have few opportunities to earn
and control cash on the island, this phenomenon becomes less surprising.
Many of these women also cultivate their own small potato fields.

The increased frequency of hiring agricultural labor does not point to the
growth of an agricultural proletariat. Most hired laborers work for others
only two or three weeks out of the year. Moreover, these workers own land
and are usually cultivators themselves. Hiring their labor out on a temporary
basis is a way to supplement their incomes.

Commodity Production

As noted above, about 80 percent of all island families are involved in
commodity production for either local or export sales, although the degree of
involvement ranges from quite small-scale to extensive (see Table 6.2). A
small number specifically produces indigenous crops (taro, sweet potatoes,
and so on), crafts, or livestock (fresh meat) to sell locally to other families or
to the schools. The example of the Tarohe family's production of *popoi*
(taro) for sale would be one instance of this. Only one family—one who
specializes in raising cattle and selling beef—earns more than $800 a month
from these types of commodity sales. Most of the rest earn less than $200 a
month.

The number of families specializing in the production and sale of
vegetables and fish is substantially larger and the earnings much higher (see
Table 6.2). Twenty-two families earn over $800 a month by selling one of
these two commodities. The demand for fresh fish, in particular by employed
families, has grown rapidly as the number of jobs and salaries has increased.
This is true because men hold most of the jobs and do all of the fishing. Most
producers of vegetables and fish, however, earn more like several hundred
dollars a month.

In general, potential earnings from commodity production are much less

Table 6.2 **Number of Households Producing Commodities and Their Average Monthly Earnings, 1987**

	Commodity				
	Vegetables	Fish	Crafts	Meat	Indigenous Crops
Income ($US)					
10–200	55	6	16	6	9
201–400	13	5	4	0	3
401–600	7	4	4	2	2
601–800	15	10	0	0	0
801–1,200	11	11	0	1	0
1,201–2,500	2	0	0	0	0
Total	103	36	24	9	14

than what a minimum-wage, government employee earns on the island. In large part this is due to Tubuai's fragile and unpredictable export market linkages. But it is also due to the essentially limited internal market for household commodities. Although the internal market has expanded greatly over the last ten years—some families now regularly purchase fish, vegetables, or other items from other families—islanders' continuing reliance on their own subsistence production and on foreign imports has constrained that expansion.

Subsistence Production

Although there is evidence to suggest that subsistence production is declining in importance in some Tubuai households, most island families continue to rely on it to meet at least half of their food needs. I believe that the most important factor contributing to the continuing importance of subsistence production is the scarcity of cash and the high costs of both local and imported foods. These high costs reflect the inflation and stiff import duties that have been features of the regional economy for decades. Prices of some of the most commonly purchased imports are as follows: small can of corned beef (340 g), $2.50; sugar (1 kg), $0.50; canned milk (410 g), $0.70; canned mackerel, $1.05; frozen chicken, $4.00/kg. Prices of some local products are: fresh fish, $3.00/kg; taro, $1.50/kg; fresh beef, $3.00/kg (1 kilogram equals about 2 pounds).

A skilled fisherman can bring home an outrigger canoe–load of fish after investing several hours of labor at sea. This canoe-load might feed a family for several weeks. On the other hand, the purchase of an equal number of kilograms of canned fish (or beef) at the store, or even the purchase of fresh fish from another fisherman, would consume a large proportion of a wage earner's monthly pay check. Islanders must also prioritize their cash expenditures. By fishing, islanders say they can avoid having to buy fish and use their cash instead to purchase Western consumer items such as radios, bicycles, and so on.

Subsistence agriculture is also attractive to islanders for other reasons. The labor requirements of subsistence production are minimal (plantations of coconuts, bananas, and papayas virtually take care of themselves) (see Joralemon 1983a), and all islanders have access to land. Taro, the major subsistence crop, is planted only in swampy areas and thus does not utilize land that might be planted with vegetables or potatoes.

In addition, islanders continue to prefer some types of indigenous cuisine to many Western foods. At feasts and on ceremonial occasions, local feast foods such as fruit puddings (*po'e*), steamed taro leaves in coconut sauce (*fafa*), and roasted pork (as well as Western foods) are expected. And finally, the household's economic security is another factor promoting the cultivation of subsistence gardens. Whereas jobs can be lost and relatively risky cash-cropping can fail, subsistence production of indigenous crops and fishing is considered to be relatively failure-proof. Thus, one can always feed one's family regardless of what economic misfortunes may occur.

One would predict that those households that relied most on subsistence production would be lower-income households and those that did not include

Men put a canoe into the water to go fishing (photo: Lockwood).

an employed member, and these predictions are substantiated by the Tubuai data (see Table 6.3). A small sample of household gardens measured in the early 1980s (N=15) indicated that middle- and high-income families (wage earners and commodity producers) cultivate on average about 110 square meters of taro per family member. Lower-income families cultivate taro patches twice that size, about 260 square meters per family member.

Table 6.3 Relative Subsistence Production of Tubuai Households by Income and Employment Status, 1987 (N=275)

	Number of Households			
	All crops[a]	Some crops[b]	None	
Income Level[c]				
Low[d]	40	4	2	
Low/middle	35	15	4	
Middle	63	31	4	
High	37	9	31	
Total	175	59	41	(275)
Employment[e]				
Not employed	104	25	6	
Employed	71	34	35	
Total	175	59	41	(275)

[a]All crops: taro, bananas, coconuts, papayas, sweet potatoes, *tarua,* and (in somes cases) manioc.
[b]Some crops: taro, bananas, coconuts, and papayas only.
[c]Chi-square=65.916; p < .001.
[d]Table 6.1 shows monetary income levels.
[e]Chi-square=28.026; p < .001.

A gradual decline in the role of subsistence production in the household economy was documented in the short span of years between 1981 and 1987 (see Table 6.4). Whereas in 1981 only 3 percent of all households surveyed did not plant subsistence gardens, by 1987 this was true of 15 percent of all households. Most of these nonplanting households were in the high-income bracket and/or included an employed member. Moreover, families now cultivate a smaller number of indigenous crops, focusing mainly on taro and tree crops and abandoning secondary cultigens such as sweet potatoes and manioc. Twenty-five percent of all families said they had reduced their subsistence gardening in the last several years, while 17 percent said they had increased theirs.

Table 6.4 Tubuai Household Subsistence Production, 1981 and 1987

| | Number of Households | | | |
	1981[a]		1987[b]	
All crops	143	(88%)	175	(64%)
Some crops	15	(9%)	59	(21%)
None	5	(3%)	41	(15%)
	163	(100%)	275	(100%)

[a]In 1981, there were approximately 200–210 households; information was gathered from 163 in the island socioeconomic census.

[b]In 1987, there were approximately 300 households; information was gathered from 275 in the island socioeconomic census.

▲ Socioeconomic Differentiation and Class

As described, island families continue to own and control their own means of production (land, mainly) and to provide most of their own labor. No class of capitalists has emerged that has concentrated control over land or the means of production. And despite the number of wage employees, no true proletariat exists. These wage earners—almost all government employees—continue to control land and other resources and usually produce commodities for sale. They do not sell their labor to capitalist enterprises but to the government. Within the context of welfare state colonialism, government employment and its high salaries are best understood as a form of transfer payment of welfare benefits and not as "wage labor" in a capitalist sense. Thus, despite capitalist market integration, class differentiation of the type usually associated with capitalism does not exist in rural Tahitian society.

Nevertheless, greater household differentiation with respect to income has taken place over the last ten years. Most significantly, government salaries have doubled and wage earners have distanced themselves from many others, not only in their level of income, but also in their Western-style consumption standards.

A comparison of household income levels (linked to occupation) in 1981 and 1987 (see Tables 6.1 and 6.5) reveals the major trends in the evolution of socioeconomic differentiation on the island. Overall, average annual income levels have increased substantially, from $4,500 in 1981 to $12,000 in 1987. Most of this is the result of the increase in government salaries. To a lesser degree it is also due to the expansion of potato and vegetable production.

Only low-income, subsistence-oriented households' income level has not risen. Low-income families were both relatively and absolutely (inflation) poorer in 1987 than they had been in 1981. It is important to note,

Table 6.5 Tubuai Households (HH): Incomes and Occupations, 1981

Socioeconomic Status (Income[a]/Occupation)	Number of HHs	% of all HHs	Share of Total Island Income (%)[b]
Low income	61	30	16
$2,000–$4,500			
(L) Subsistence			
Low/middle income	9	4	2
$2,000–$5,000			
(L/M) Pension			
Middle income			44
$4,500–$7,000			
(M1) Markets	21	10	
(M2) Employed	73	35	
High income			38
$7,000–$15,000			
(H0) Skilled employment	17	8	
(H1) Dual employment	9	4	
(H2) Markets/employment	11	5	
(H3) Major marketer	5	2	
Total	206	98	100

Note: The figures on household income were compiled from household census data and budgets and from information furnished by employers and local government agencies. There may be as much as a 5 percent error in the mean.

[a]All figures are in U.S. dollars ($). In 1981, one U.S. dollar was equivalent to 75 Communautés Françaises du Pacifique (CFP) francs; in 1987, 100 CFP francs equaled $1.00.

[b]Calculations were made by multiplying the mean annual income (left-hand column) by the number of households in that category, and then dividing by the total number of households.

however, that there were fewer low-income families in 1987 than in 1981. This decline reflects the movement of some previously low-income families into potato cultivation and other small-scale commodity production, and the participation of others in the government's new retirement pension program for the non–formally employed.

In the late 1980s, there was not only a larger number of wealthy, high-income families, but they controlled a significantly greater proportion of total island income (38 percent in 1981 versus 53 percent in 1987). Most of these were government employees.

In general, wage-earning families are not interested in primary production and do little with their land other than cultivate small patches of taro and tree crops and a small garden of potatoes during the winter months. They do not invest their sizable incomes in local enterprise but mostly consume it on imported consumer luxuries. Although it is relatively wealthy and is an increasingly observable social category in island society, this elite does not constitute a class of capitalists because they do not invest their wealth, transforming it into capital, nor do they possess differential control of the means of production or hire labor.

▲ Evolving Tubuai Households

During the change-filled years between 1980 and 1991, I had the opportunity to watch the growth and economic evolution of many island families. The Tarohe family's economic roller coaster ride described in the previous chapter illustrates the impact of the uncertainties of large-scale vegetable cultivation on the families who specialized in this activity. The following additional household profiles highlight other diverse ways in which Tubuai's households participate in the peasant mode of production on the island.

The Tane Household

In 1981, the Tanes were a high-income, wage-earning family that dabbled in commodity production, cultivated subsistence gardens, and fished. Tere was 48 years old and his wife, Vaite, was 41. They had had six children; the three eldest daughters worked and lived in Papeete, while the three younger children (16, 15, and 9) were at home. The couple had also adopted two smaller children, one grandson and the son of a cousin, who were 8 and 5. Thus, the household included two adults and five children. Tere had been married previously but his wife had died; they had had a son (François) and daughter, both of whom lived with their families in Papeete.

The Tane household was located on Tere's family land. Nearby were the households of his father (who lived with one of his daughters), a sister, and a brother. Each cultivated separate taro patches along the stream that ran through the familial property, as well as separate vegetable gardens.

Both Tere and Vaite were employed, he as a maintenance man for the municipality and she as a part-time cook at the primary school. Together they earned about $650 a month in salaries in 1981. They kept separate bank accounts where their salaries were deposited. Vaite's account was used to buy food and other necessities for the family, while Tere's account was used to make the loan payments on a truck they had purchased in 1979.

The Tanes also cultivated a vegetable garden (900 square meters) mostly for household consumption, but they sold any surplus (about 10–15 kg/week) at the Saturday morning market at the *mairie*. Tere had first cultivated vegetables on a large scale in the 1960s after having returned to Tubuai from a job in the Makatea phosphate mines. When he found full-time work with the municipality in the early 1970s, he gave up vegetable production. The small household garden was mainly cultivated by Vaite and one of her daughters. The Tanes also sold prepared foods (Tahitian puddings and other specialties cooked in an *umu*) each week at the Saturday market. If Tere and his son Teiura had caught a surplus of fish, this would also be sold. On a typical Saturday, the family might earn $30–$50.

The family also gathered coffee from familial plantations (selling 50 kg in 1981 and consuming the rest), and Vaite made and sold sandwiches at the high school soccer matches held each Sunday (earning about $20 each Sunday). The family received about $100 per month in family allocations. Overall, their average monthly income was about $900 in 1981.

In addition to their cash-earning activities, the family cultivated taro (1,100 square meters) and other subsistence crops (manioc, sweet potatoes, etc.), relying on subsistence production (fish, too) for much of the foods they consumed. The eldest son occasionally worked in a *pupu* with his cousins to prepare the taro patches for planting. The family also kept two cows and numerous chickens.

In 1979, the Tane family were making monthly payments of about $240 on their truck loan. They had received an agricultural subsidy to purchase the truck, which offset almost half of its price. The payments on the truck, plus gasoline (about $200 a month) consumed about 40 percent of their total monthly cash income.

The family also owned a motor for their canoe and an electric generator, which they used almost exclusively to run a freezer where they stored fish. The generator was also used occasionally to run household lights for several hours each evening. Although the family owned a gas stove, most cooking was done over an outside cook fire or in the earth oven.

The Tane family were not only economically active, but also they were active in community affairs. Tere was a lay pastor in the Sanito church, and Vaite was president of the women's church group. Tere was also president of the district branch of his political party. Like many other prominent people, neither Tere or Vaite had had more than two or three years of primary school education and neither spoke French well.

By 1985, the salary earnings of Tere and Vaite had increased substantially. Together they now earned about $1,700 a month. They still cultivated their small vegetable garden, but exclusively for household consumption; the Saturday market had been disbanded several years before. To supplement their incomes they were now making Tahitian doughnuts (*firifiris*) early Sunday mornings to sell to people who came to the house (the Chinese stores also sell *firifiris* Sunday mornings); they earned about $80–$100 each Sunday.

By 1985, electricity had been installed in their district, and the family had had to pay about $2,000 for the poles and wiring needed to reach their house from the road. Vaite was especially pleased to no longer have to crank the old generator by hand. The house had also been remodeled. A new, Western-style kitchen (with appliances) and two indoor bathrooms had been added (the old outhouse was still used on occasion), and Western-style furniture and a television set had been purchased.

In 1983, Tere's son Teiura had been called to do his military service and was stationed in France for a year. The previous year a young woman he had been seeing gave birth to a son and Vaite had adopted the baby. Teiura had not wanted to return to Tubuai after his year of service, preferring to remain in France. His father, however, insisted that he return as he was "his only son" and Tere could not manage the work in the gardens and fishing without him. Apparently Tere did not think that his two younger adopted sons would stay on the family land once they became young adults.

After his return, Teiura took on the major responsibility for the potatoes the family had started planting in the early 1980s (1,000 kg in 1983), and he was given a portion of the income by his father. Teiura also sold fish and small quantities of vegetables he cultivated to make money for himself. In 1985, he met his cousin's wife's sister, who was visiting from the neighboring island of Raivavae. After eating a meal together at a church dinner (which everyone took be a significant public announcement), she returned with him to his parents' house to live as his wife.

Between 1981 and 1985, Hina, the eldest teenage daughter, had gone to Papeete to attend three years of a secretarial school run by the Sanito church. Unable to find a job in Papeete, she returned to Tubuai in 1985 hoping to start a dressmaking "boutique" business on Tubuai.

In 1983, Tere's eldest son (by his first marriage), François (35 years old), returned to live on Tubuai with his family after an absence of almost fifteen years. François had been employed as a construction worker and his wife as a cook in a hotel in Papeete; they earned about $1,400 a month. Like other returning migrant families, they had never seriously considered coming home to Tubuai until they found that they were having a difficult time supporting their growing family in Papeete. They had had nine children in the twelve years they had been married. After paying rent and buying food, they had nothing left at the end of the month.

François had benefited from government aids to families who would return to their outer-island homes and was given financial help (about $3,000) to build a small plyboard house on Tubuai. It was built on family lands across the stream from his father's house. François began immediately to plant potatoes and vegetables, hoping to make his living as a commercial farmer; in 1987, he was earning about $500 a month. Although their total income had declined after the return to Tubuai, the family was no longer paying rent and was producing most of its own food. Both François and his wife felt that their lives had improved and they had great expectations for the future.

Although Tere had encouraged François to return to Tubuai, the large extended Tane family (Tere's siblings and their children) was utilizing almost all of its available familial lands. Unfortunately for the present generation, Tere's father had sold one large parcel to the government about twenty years earlier. François had had to go his mother's family to ask to use some land near the road that had never been previously cleared or planted. He obtained that permission after a lengthy family dispute; François believed that his mother's family was jealous of him and resented their loss of potential access to the land. To discourage him from wanting to cultivate the parcel, they had told him that *tupapa'u* (ghosts) gathered near the old abandoned familial house on the property and that his cultivation efforts would never succeed. François chose to ignore the stories and went ahead with his plans.

After several years, Teina, François's wife, decided to cultivate her own potato fields. She had wanted to buy a sewing machine for some time and François had not been willing to give her the money. She, as well as the children, had worked extensively in François's fields, but she had decided to sign up to cultivate in her own name and use the earned money as she pleased. She planted a section of land adjacent to François's.

In 1987, Tere bought a new Toyota truck (also with government aid), and the Tane family gave every appearance of being the prosperous family they were. Vaite no longer wore the homemade dresses she had sewn in the early 1980s (from Tahitian print *pareu* fabric purchased at the Chinese store), but instead wore ready-made, Western-style dresses she purchased in Papeete when she visited family members there.

By 1991, Vaite's and Tere's salaries had risen and they were now earning about $2,100 a month. But Tere expected to retire the next year when he turned 60, and to start receiving a pension. Between 1987 and 1991, he had aged significantly and was now known for the argumentative (and frequently irrational) diatribes he frequently delivered during church meetings. Some of the members of the congregation attributed his lapses to a time many years earlier when he had been sorcerized by a jealous older sister (who had caused the deaths of several infants) and had acted quite strangely for several days.

Tere hoped that when he retired, his son Teiura would be able to assume his job. Teiura was barely making a living (and supporting his growing family) by cultivating potatoes and by selling surplus fish each week. After being pressured by his father, Teiura and his wife had been married in the Sanito church in 1987 and they now had four children. In 1991, they had almost completed a small house constructed behind Tere and Vaite's. Tere's share of his father's familial land had been informally divided among three of his children, including Teiura. The other children would receive portions of their mother's land.

By 1991, the Tane family's vegetable gardens had largely been taken over by a teenaged son and daughter (then 18 and 17 years old), who planted green peppers. In 1990, they had earned money by selling (for export) about two tons to the agricultural cooperative. The family's subsistence gardens (mainly taro) had been reduced by about half, and they were consuming more imported food.

What stood out in particular about the Tane family over the years was that although Tere and Vaite together earned a high income, the consumption goals of this ever-expanding family always exceeded its income. To supplement their salaries they also sold surplus household production and actively pursued numerous small cash-earning activities.

The Haramea Family

In 1981, the Haramea family was typical of many low-income, subsistence-oriented families. Nani (30 years old) and Iotefa (39 years old) first met when she was 15 (in 1966), and they soon began staying together at his sister's house. After the birth of several children they acceded to the wishes of their Mormon pastor and were legally married. They had five children, one of whom was given away in *fa'a'amu*. Nani felt that five children were enough, and following the birth of her last child she began using the birth control offered by the island clinic. Although many women want to limit the number of children they bear, Nani was among a small group who had actually agreed to use birth control.

In the late 1970s, Iotefa had gone to work on a cargo ship for several years to earn enough money to build their own house. It was built on family lands near his sister's house and was almost completed in 1981. The family had just moved into it when I first met them. Because they had no money for furnishings, the house remained largely empty, with the exception of several beds, pandanus mats, and wooden crates, where clothing and other items were stored.

Iotefa was not interested in trying to get a job on Tubuai or in cultivating cash crops. He complained that he was unable to do heavy labor because of a previous back injury. Nani said he was lazy, although she herself had no interest in planting either vegetables or potatoes. She said it was too expensive to plant potatoes; she cited the high costs of seed potatoes, fertilizers, and insecticides. They did cultivate a large area (1,600 square meters) of taro, but in contrast to general patterns, it was Nani and a women's *pupu* who performed most of the cultivation labor. The family also kept three pigs, whose litters were fattened and sold for extra money.

Iotefa fished several times a week, and earnings from sales of surplus fish brought in most of the family's cash income. In 1981, Nani took the fish to each Saturday morning market and earned about $20–$40 per week. She also made pandanus and *ni'au* (coconut fiber) crafts—mats, hats, and satchels—selling one occasionally at the Mataura craft association where she was a member. Family allocations also brought in about $200 a month.

In all, the family earned about $300–$400 a month in 1981. Each year the Harameas also gathered coffee from familial plantations; in 1986, they had earned $300 in coffee sales. They purchased a few imported foods at the Chinese stores, but produced close to 90 percent of all the food they consumed. They had scraped together the money to buy a used Vespa motorbike, which was their sole means of transportation. It was common to see either Nani or Iotefa, and at least two children, perched precariously atop the Vespa on their way to town.

In 1981, Nani and Iotefa's 15-year-old daughter, Rava, had left school and Nani had agreed to let Rava's boyfriend stay with her at the house. Nani was nevertheless outraged to learn that her daughter was pregnant. The relationship with the boyfriend did not last, and when Rava's child was born, Nani reluctantly adopted it, saying that she was too old to have to care for another baby.

When I returned in 1985, I was surprised to learn that Nani and Iotefa had started cultivating potatoes in 1982. By this time, many low-income, subsistence-oriented families had begun participating in the development project. Nani explained that they had helped Iotefa's sister in her potato fields and that although the costs were high, she felt confident that they could make money (as his sister had). Iotefa and Nani did not agree, however, on how their potato earnings would be used, so they each cultivated their own potato field and kept the money in separate bank accounts.

In 1982 and 1983, each had planted 500 kg of seed potatoes, raising it to 1,000 kg in the following years. Nani claims that in 1984 she earned $2,000 after expenses. Iotefa and Nani cultivated land that actually belonged to two of Iotefa's siblings who lived in Papeete. The family had informally divided their holdings among themselves, although the legal land registration had never taken place.

In 1986, Iotefa died unexpectedly from a heart attack while spearfishing (by some miracle his young son was able to lift his large body into the canoe and return to shore). Unfortunately, the death took place not long after a family dispute in which his cousin, an elderly woman who lived nearby on family lands, claimed that he had stolen some cash from her house. He had been seen loitering near the house, and not long after the money's disappearance, Iotefa had somehow (also miraculously) gotten together enough money to buy a new freezer. There was some talk that the death had been caused by sorcery, revenge on the part of the elderly woman. But the elderly woman herself went to great pains to reassure others that she could never have been involved in something like that. Since she was well liked and known for her many kindnesses to others, no one believed that she had promoted his death. Indeed, although Iotefa had had no previous heart problems, he was quite overweight and his claims to ill health were well known by all.

Nani was not sure how she would support the family alone. The previous year, Rava had married (in Papeete) a young man employed by the nuclear testing facilities on the island of Mururoa. Because families are not allowed to accompany Mururoa employees, Rava decided to return to Tubuai with her second and third child when she learned of her father's death. She received money from her husband each month and began helping her mother financially. Rava and her husband planned to build a small house next to Nani's as soon as possible.

Nani continued to cultivate potatoes and to sell her crafts, and she had also started to plant carrots. In 1986, she sold several tons to a local entrepreneur for export to Papeete. In 1987, her total earnings were about $5,000.

By 1991, Nani's situation had improved. Rava's husband had found a job as a carpenter at the public works service on Tubuai and they had completed their house. Although Nani continued to grow potatoes each season (500 kg only) and occasionally to sell the craft items she wove, Rava helped her financially by paying her electricity bill and by buying major items she needed, including a washing machine. Nani also received some money from one of her other daughters who lived in Papeete. Nani had agreed to care for this daughter's two small children (not exactly *fa'a'amu*) while the daughter worked and sent Nani money for food and other necessities.

In addition to the salary (about $2,000 a month) her husband brought in, Rava cultivated potatoes and carrots on a small scale. She earned several thousand dollars this way each year, but put the money in a joint account with her husband. She said that she and her husband made all major decisions about the family and expenditures together. In addition to taking part in a women's *pupu* that produced large mats and did other work, she was a major organizer of the fundraising activities of the Mormon church to which she belonged. Rava frequently felt overburdened by her many domestic and community activities.

Essentially, the families of mother and daughter had been merged into one, although they lived in separate houses several hundred meters apart. Since Nani had no regular source of income other than small-scale potato cultivation (she considered her other sources of income to be temporary), she could not support herself and her dependents. As she said, her daughter's husband had become their "papa" now.

▲ 7
Islanders and Capitalism: The Tubuai Potato Project

The prevalence of the peasant mode of production in many developing Third World communities has been an issue of great interest to anthropologists and other social scientists. Once it was recognized that this mode of production was not transitional between "traditional" economic forms and capitalist relations of production, scholars began to investigate the forces that might be responsible for its evolution and persistence throughout the Third World.

Some dependency and world systems theorists argue that the peasant mode of production is actually the creation of capitalism, and that it is linked to the chronic rural underdevelopment and economic stagnation characteristic of many Third World societies (see Frank 1966; Wallerstein 1974). Marxist scholars specifically propose that rural underdevelopment is perpetuated because the peasant household is exploited by capitalists who retain the surplus value of the peasants' products and labor. Because peasants are paid as little as possible for the market commodities they produce (or the labor they sell) by profit-seeking capitalists, they are unable to accumulate capital, to reinvest in production, and to raise their standard of living.

According to this perspective, because the peasant household has little income, it must continue to fulfill many of its own needs through subsistence production. This prevents the household from allocating more of its capital resources and labor to market production and thus from increasing its income. But ironically, because the household is fulfilling some of its own needs, capitalists pay peasants less for their products or labor (they still will not starve), and in this way subsistence production operates as a subsidy for the capitalist.

In light of these exploitation-oriented arguments, the persistence of the peasant mode of production in rural Tahitian society is particularly interesting. As noted earlier, considering islanders' high standard of living and affluence, as well as the general context of welfare state colonialism, it is difficult to consider rural Tahitians exploited. They certainly do not experience the usual consequences of exploitation—impoverishment, an inability to accumulate capital, and so on. According to the theoretical arguments, it is these consequences that promote the maintenance of traditional, noncapitalist relations of production. Thus, the case of rural Tahitian society suggests that there are particular conditions or factors other than capitalist exploitation per se that perpetuate this socioeconomic form (at least in some areas of the world).

Examining the Tubuai case, it appears that the peasant mode of production is a phenomenon that has evolved as islanders have interacted with their particular economic linkages. Part of that interaction is shaped by conditions operating in the regional and world capitalist economies— conditions largely beyond the control of rural Tahitians. The risky nature of green vegetable cultivation and export, for example, is the product of Papeete market conditions and has little to do with Tubuai farmers. A few island families, like the Tarohes, are willing to undertake these risks, while most are not.

But islanders' interactions with their market linkages—specifically, how they participate in commodity production and agricultural development programs—are also influenced by factors internal to island society and by factors internal to the organization of rural Tahitian households. These factors are related to Tahitian patterns of sociocultural organization and social interaction. They are also related to islanders' values, perceptions, goals, and strategies for fulfilling those goals.

One cannot, however, identify *a* Tubuai response to capitalism. As the earlier examples of Tubuai households have shown, island families are highly heterogeneous and participate in different ways and to different degrees in economic development. This variability is related to interhousehold differences in circumstances and worldview. Tubuai families have different resource endowments (land, labor, capital, etc.), as well as different aspirations and value orientations. Some are relatively richer or poorer, older or younger (stage in the developmental cycle of the family), larger or smaller, or more or less oriented toward Western-style consumption. They also belong to different religious denominations and thus have different outlooks on many issues.

Moreover, as in every society, but particularly in rapidly Westernizing societies, the goals and worldview of older and younger people are significantly different. Older people may remember and value the more traditional ways of the premodernization era, while young people do not. And in every society, men and women differ significantly in the roles they play in the household and community, in their ability to make decisions, in their access to and control over resources, and in their personal goals.

These differences play a critical role in shaping islanders' diverse economic choices and behaviors. One must expect that particular households and specific segments of the community will perceive, value, and participate differently in available opportunities and in change.

One can achieve important insights into the factors that shape Tubuai islanders' economic behaviors by analyzing their differential involvement in potato cultivation. In the process of understanding how islanders choose to interact with capitalism in the context of this particular development project, one can also achieve important insights into the forces internal to rural Tahitian society that are actively supporting and reinforcing the peasant mode of production.

▲ Patterns of Participation in 1981

In 1980, approximately two years after the start of the potato project, only forty-one farmers (representing 20 percent of all households) were cultivating potatoes (see Table 7.1). Most of these farmers earned middle and high incomes and were oriented toward market production (i.e., M1, H2, H3), as opposed to wage labor (see Table 7.1). Although the household head may also have held a job, production of a marketable surplus was an important feature of potato-cultivating households' economic endeavors.

It was surprising for a number of reasons that other segments of the population were not participating in the project. First, islanders had access to land, and most, even the employed, sought ways to increase or supplement

Table 7.1 Potato Cultivation by Households of Different Socioeconomic Status, 1981 and 1987

Socioeconomic Status (Income/Occupation)	Potato Cultivation 1980 (N=206)			Potato Cultivation 1987 (N=284)		
	No	Yes	% Participation	No	Yes	% Participation
(L) Low Income: Subsistence	54	7	11	3	43	93
(L/M) Low/middle income: pension	9	0	0	33	25	43
(M1) Middle income: Markets	10	11	52	5	22	81
(M2) Middle income: Unskilled employment	63	10	14	12	60	83
(H0) High income: Skilled employment	16	1	6	13	22	63
(H1) High income: Dual employment	8	1	1	12	12	50
(H2) High income: Markets/employment	4	7	64	2	11	85
(H3) High income: Major marketer	1	4	80	0	9	100
Total	165	41	20	80	204	72

their incomes. In a successful season, potato cultivation could be lucrative; a one-hectare planter could earn as much as $2,300 (after expenses) for three months of labor. At the scale that most farmers planted (500–1,500 kg of seed potatoes, or 0.2–0.5 hectare), family labor was sufficient. As noted previously, cultivation costs were heavily subsidized (at 60 percent) by the government, and credit was available to cover incurred costs until harvest. Moreover, purchase of the entire crop, marketing, and transport were all guaranteed.

Potato farming did, however, involve some cultivation uncertainty. Much of the island is low-lying and swampy and islanders cannot predict the highly variable rains and storms that quickly inundate fields. Insect infestations are also highly unpredictable from season to season. In 1981, about 15 percent of all farmers did not earn enough to repay their costs and went into debt. In an average year, between 5 and 15 percent of all farmers lose money.

Low-income families, 16 percent of all island families (see Table 6.5), were notably absent from the project. Since capital was not required to start planting and these families might be looking for ways to augment their income, one might expect higher rates of participation.

Interviews with low-income families indicated that their hesitation to participate in the project was linked to their perceptions of the risks involved and the implications for them of going into debt. Although capital was not required to plant, low-income families were greatly concerned with how "expensive" seed potatoes and other inputs were. Relative to other families, they were also highly sensitive to the potential for incurring a debt.

For low-income families, losses in a bad season would mean that they would be unable to maintain the relatively high and culturally defined "minimum subsistence standard" (Wharton 1971) on the island. This included purchases of imported foods and consumer items, which had become "necessities" in the island's artificially inflated standard of living. In contrast, middle- and high-income families could sustain losses and not have their minimum subsistence standard jeopardized. The strong relationship between perceptions of risk, innovation, and socioeconomic rank in developing communities has been documented previously (Cancian 1972, 1979; Dewalt 1975).

Low rates of potato cultivation among other segments of the population, particularly pensioners (L/M households) and high-income households that focus on wage employment (H0 and H1 households) (see Table 7.1), did not appear to be surprising. Pensioners were usually elderly, and households that included a skilled wage earner or two wage-earning spouses rarely undertook commodity production on any significant scale.

In 1981, the small group of market-oriented and relatively high-income potato farmers were rapidly expanding production, obtaining use rights to larger areas of family land, and earning sizable amounts of money. Large-scale farmers were earning incomes (in three months) equal to the yearly salaries of wage earners (about $4,500). Between 1979 and 1981, the average scale of production had more than doubled, from 1,050 kg to 2,470 kg of seed potatoes planted (see Table 7.2). While entrepreneurial farmers were expanding, few new farmers had joined the project; between 1979 and 1981 only seven new farmers had started potato cultivation (forty farmers in 1979 and forty-seven in 1981—see Table 7.2).

Table 7.2 Tubuai Potato Cultivation, 1979–1990

Year	Number of Planters	Seed Potatoes Planted (kg)	Total Production (kg)	Average Amount Planted per Cultivator (kg)
1979	40	42,000	117,700	1,050
1980	41	68,000	224,000	1,660
1981	47	116,000	379,000	2,470
1982	90	105,600	501,000	1,170
1983	102	126,800	545,000	1,240
1984	135	152,000	738,000	1,130
1985	172	165,000	791,000	960
1986	217	215,000	941,500	990
1987	264	280,000	1,370,000	1,060
1988–1990	270	280,000	1,200,000	1,000

Source: Service de l'Économie Rurale, Tubuai, French Polynesia.
Note: Tubuai cultivators plant approximately 2,500 to 3,000 kg of seed potatoes per hectare of land. Thus, approximately 1,200 to 1,500 kg of seed potatoes would be planted on 0.5 hectare.

Thus, it appeared in 1981 that differential participation in potato cultivation was not only laying the foundations for increasing social inequalities, but also promoting the structural changes commensurate with the transformation to local-level capitalism. As this small group of profit-oriented farmers expanded, they would create increasing pressure on land and seek to achieve unilateral control over it. If land divisions took place, these farmers could purchase land and eventually concentrate control over some of the best agricultural parcels. Those families not significantly involved in agriculture or commodity production (wage earners and low-income families) would be motivated to sell land to acquire money. Potato farmers could easily become the major landowners on the island. Those who had sold their land would then be required to either work for the government or migrate to Papeete to find jobs, or they could become paid farmworkers (proletariats) for the island's large-scale potato cultivators (who would need the labor).

The general scenario that has just been described is one that has taken place on the main island of Tahiti as well as in other regions of the developing world. In particular, development appears to be strongly linked to increasing community wealth differences and structured social inequality (e.g., Finney 1973; Cancian 1972; Epstein 1962; Pelto and Pelto 1973; Firth 1946; Roseberry 1976). Studies by anthropologists have documented a recurring pattern: Small segments of the community differentially benefit from development, become wealthy, and, in some cases, are able to concentrate control over land or the other means of production (see Smith 1980). In contrast, the majority benefits little, if at all, and may be either relatively or absolutely worse off after development.

▲ The Demise of Capitalist Farming: Patterns of Participation in 1987

By 1987, however, this projected scenario had not taken place on Tubuai, nor was there even movement in that direction. By the late 1980s, potato cultivation had become a widespread activity of the vast majority of island households. Seventy-two percent of all households cultivated; there were 264 planters representing 204 of the islands' approximately 300 households.[1] In some cases, more than one member of a household (i.e., a husband and wife, a father and son) cultivated his or her own independent fields.

Furthermore, the dramatic increase in the number of potato farmers occurred across all socioeconomic strata and segments of the Tubuai population. Whereas only 11 percent of low-income families cultivated in 1981, 93 percent of this group were cultivating in 1987. Women had begun cultivating potatoes independently and constituted one-third of all planters in 1987; by 1990 they were 43 percent of all planters. Moreover, the rate of new female cultivators joining the project in every year after 1981 was higher than that for new male cultivators (Lockwood 1989:198). Return migrant families were also playing an unexpectedly significant role in potato cultivation. By the late 1980s, over half of all Tubuai potato planters were either women, return migrants, or members of low-income households.

In addition to the dramatic change in participation patterns, the average scale of cultivation had declined by more than half (from 2,470 kg to 1,060 kg of seed potatoes—see Table 7.2). Of the twenty-one farmers who had cultivated on the largest scale in 1981 (greater than 1,500 kg of seed potatoes, about 0.5 hectare), fifteen had left the program or reduced their scale of cultivation (see Table 7.3).

Many of the large-scale farmers had experienced financial losses due to weather, poor soils, insects, or shortages of labor as they had tried to expand. Considering the island's terrain and other production conditions, as well as the large financial investment required, cultivation in excess of about one hectare had proven to be highly risky.

Table 7.3 Scale of Potato Cultivation, 1980–1981 and 1987

| Kilograms of Seed Potatoes Planted | Number of Cultivators | | | |
| | 1980–1981 | | 1987 | |
	N	%	N	%
< 500	5	12	108	41
500–1,500	15	37	120	45
1,500–3,000	14	34	28	11
> 3,000	7	17	8	3
Total	41	100	264	100

Note: Approximately 2,500–3,000 kg of seed potatoes are planted per hectare.

One Tubuai man, for example, began potato cultivation in 1985 by ambitiously planting four tons of seed potatoes. In a disastrous season, he harvested only nine tons and took on a sizable debt. He had planted his crop on his wife's family land not more than fifty meters from the ocean. Strong winds off the ocean, as well as heavy rains that season, damaged the young plants. He planned to plant only one ton of seed potatoes the next year. Despite his losses, he was still optimistic in 1985 about vegetable cultivation in general and had plans to make a great deal of money as a commercial farmer. But when I returned to Tubuai in 1987, he had given up potato cultivation altogether and gone to Papeete to help relatives build a house. His wife and two teenage daughters had remained on the island and in 1987 were planting their own potatoes, but on a much reduced scale (500 kg of seed potatoes).

By 1987, the average scale of potato cultivation on the island was about 0.2–0.3 hectare (500–750 kg seed potatoes); income earned in an average season (after expenses) was about $1,000. In part, the withdrawal of some expansionist farmers and reduction of scale by others had eased the way for numerous small planters to move into the project by reducing competition for land.

Although many large-scale farmers cultivating in 1981 had either left the program or reduced their scale of cultivation, it should be noted that there were, in absolute numbers, more large-scale farmers (planting more than 1,500 kg) in 1987 than in 1981 (see Table 7.3). Many of the large-scale farmers in 1987 had adopted potato cultivation only the preceding few years; a number of these farmers were return migrants or young household heads. Whether or not many of these relatively new potato cultivators would withdraw or reduce their scale (as earlier large-scale farmers had) remained to be seen.

The small scale of production chosen by the vast majority of cultivators in the late 1980s meant that potatoes were not a major source of income for most families (see Table 7.4). Indeed, the significance of potato earnings for most families had declined significantly. In 1981, they constituted on average 30–50 percent of household income, while in 1987 potato earnings made up only about 10–25 percent of household income for those who planted (see Table 7.4).

Table 7.4 Percentage of Total Income Earned Through Potato Cultivation, 1981 and 1987

1981 (Average planted = 2,500 kg)[a]

Income Level	Number of Households	% of Income
Low (mean $3,250)	7	62–92
Middle (mean $5,750)	21	35–52
High (mean $11,000)	13	18–27

1987 (Average planted = 1,000 kg)[b]

Income Level	Number of Households	% of Income
Low (mean $3,250)	68	31–46
Middle (mean $12,000)	82	8–13
High (mean $25,000)	54	4–6

[a]Average earnings (after expenses) estimated to be $2,000–$3,000.
[b]Average earnings (after expenses) estimated to be $1,000–$1,500.

It is important to note that the shift to a pattern of multiple, small-scale cultivations was not associated with declining efficiency or productivity. Yields steadily increased between 1981 and 1987 (SER 1981–1987), and production jumped from 380 metric tons in 1981 to 1,370 tons in 1987 and then stabilized at about 1,200 tons for marketing reasons.

▲ Push Factors and Small-Scale, Household-Based Potato Cultivation

If large-scale potato cultivation had proven to be feasible on the island, it is likely that "capitalist" agriculture would have expanded. But large-scale farming required a willingness to undertake substantial financial risks; production conditions were highly variable (weather, etc.), and large-scale farming stretched family labor to its limit, requiring paid labor, which was difficult to find. Because potatoes require a great deal of hand labor for planting, mounding, spraying insecticides, weeding, and harvesting, few large-scale farmers are able to maintain their fields as well as they should to promote high yields. In addition, large-scale farming may also stretch use rights to family land to their limit. Larger parcels may simply not be available, or kin may also demand their rights to use particular parcels.

Moreover, by 1991, it was clear that Tubuai potato production could no longer expand. As mentioned previously, in 1987 farmers had produced a record 1,370 tons, and 170 of those tons had rotted because they could not be marketed. Tubuai can grow potatoes only during its three cool winter months, and so most of the Tubuai potato crop falls on Papeete markets within the short span of several months. Papeete markets simply cannot absorb all of it. By 1991, agricultural officials had put the cap on production at 1,200 tons. Thus, marketing considerations also limit the expansion of commercial agriculture on the island.

Push Factors

While the efforts of large-scale farmers to concentrate landholdings and expand production were frequently meeting with failure, other segments of the population that had played no previous role in the development project began to plant potatoes in unprecedented numbers and on an almost uniformly small scale. Certainly, demonstration effects were at work. Noncultivators had watched (and helped) members of their families or neighbors plant and harvest potatoes during the preceding years. Most often, harvests were successful and island families made money. Noncultivators would have gained both knowledge of potato cultivation and confidence to undertake it themselves.

I do not believe, however, that demonstration effects were sufficient to bring about the phenomenal increase in participation in the potato project. This is true for two reasons. First, noncultivators would be just as likely to observe that cultivation was risky and could lead to debt in a bad season. And second, the trend toward rapidly increasing participation did not materialize until some years into the project. Typically, demonstration effects begin to work after one or two successful seasons.

Statements made by many new potato farmers suggest instead that they were pushed into potato cultivation by factors appearing on the Tubuai scene during the 1980s. These factors effectively brought entire segments of the population into the project—segments that had been notably absent from it in the first half of the decade: low-income families, women, return migrants, and young people.

Low-Income Families

Although hesitant to undertake financial risks, low-income families (mostly subsistence oriented) were, I believe, pushed into cultivation by rapidly rising consumption standards and an increase in their relative poverty since the early 1980s. In short, they needed to earn more money. Between 1981 and 1987, the salaries of government wage earners had doubled (from $400 to $800 a month); this was linked to a rapidly rising cost of living and inflation throughout the territory. With new opportunities in commodity production, middle- and high-income non–wage earning families were also earning significantly higher incomes by the end of the decade. In 1981, the average annual familial income was $4,500 and in 1987, $12,000. Only low-income families had experienced no increase in their overall income levels during these years. In relative terms, they were poorer than they had been in 1981 (and poorer still considering inflation). In the late 1980s, they earned a smaller share of total island income than they had in 1981 (1981, 16 percent; 1987, 4 percent; see Tables 6.1 and 6.5).

As described earlier, with the installation of electricity on the island during these years, islanders' consumption of imports and manufactured goods escalated sharply. The culturally defined minimum subsistence standard had risen to include a television set and other consumer items generally beyond the reach of low-income families. Because potato cultivation required no capital outlays to start planting, it was a particularly accessible option for low-income families to increase their incomes.

Return Migrants

Return migrant families had also moved into potato cultivation by the late 1980s. Many of the thirty-six families who returned to the island between 1981 and 1987 hoped to find jobs on Tubuai and/or take advantage of commercial agriculture opportunities. The latter proved to be easier than the former because of the limited number of government jobs. For the most part, however, these families were not experienced cultivators. Many of them opted to participate in the potato program and benefit from government subsidies and aid instead of attempting to go into other kinds of commodity production (e.g., green vegetables) that were more risky. Eighty-three percent of return migrant families, in contrast to 69 percent of all other households, were planting potatoes.

In many ways, the experiences of Titaha and his family exemplified those of many return migrant families. I first met Titaha in 1985—he had returned to Tubuai in 1982 when his elderly father had died, leaving him the ancient familial house and land (which he actually co-owned with an absent brother and sister). Titaha had left Tubuai when he was 14 and had earned his living in Papeete in various ways, including working as an auto mechanic for minimum wage. Although Titaha claims that he returned because of his father's last words, "Never forget your true country" (i.e., Tubuai), one guesses that Titaha, his wife, and their six children were having a hard time making ends meet in Papeete.

Titaha had hoped to find a job on Tubuai and when that failed, he started a small car repair business; lacking parts and equipment, it too soon failed. He was then able to find a two-day-a-week job as a gardener for the Mormon church (to which he belonged) in his district. In addition to his salary of about $370 a month, he began planting potatoes (in 1983) and subsistence gardens (taro, etc.) and fished several times a week, selling his surplus to neighboring families. His income in 1985 was about $7,000 a year. He had two good potato seasons in 1984 and 1985 and increased his quantity of seed potatoes from 500 kg to 1,000 kg in 1986. He wanted desperately to make money so that his family could move out of the crumbling familial house and build a new house.

When I returned to the island in 1987, little had changed for Titaha. In addition to his part-time job, he still relied on potatoes for an important supplement to his income. Although he had envisioned expanding production beyond the 1,000 kg, he had abandoned the idea because of a shortage of familial labor. All of his children were in school, and his wife, a woman from Papeete, did not want to work in the *faaapu* (fields) like Tubuai women. Titaha had gotten some help by participating in a Mormon *pupu,* a group of Mormons who worked cooperatively in each other's potato fields.

Many return migrant families like Titaha's may be pushed into potato cultivation, especially when they cannot find wage employment.

Women Cultivators

One can also argue that factors related to Tahitian patterns of gender stratification and women's subordinate socioeconomic position pushed them into potato cultivation at what proved to be an astounding rate. Most female cultivators said that they had decided to become potato farmers because they wanted to earn their own money and to achieve some financial autonomy in the male-dominated household. Because women had access to land and the potato project required no capital to start planting (something few women had), potato cultivation was an accessible income-earning option for them. This is discussed at greater length in the next chapter.

Young People

Young people, including unmarried sons and daughters still living with parents, had also started planting potatoes in large numbers. To receive cultivation loans through SOCREDO, cultivators had to be at least 18 years of age. A young man or woman would ask for a portion of family land and start cultivating to earn his or her own money. Usually the young person had a specific purchase in mind, such as a motorcycle; or he or she might be earning money for Papeete school expenses or a future house. Young people today have numerous personal consumption goals, and they cannot count on their families to give them the money for all of the expensive imported luxuries they covet (e.g., Walkman stereos, electric guitars, and so on). In addition, newly married young couples without a job or other established source of income frequently turned to potato cultivation because they had few other ways to make money.

Taking up potato cultivation and becoming a farmer stands in stark contrast to the stated aspirations and career goals of most island young people. Many would like to become professionals, with high-paying and prestigious jobs. But in reality, few have the necessary education to reach these goals. Their actual options for making a living are limited. It is difficult to find a job on the island, and there are long waiting lists for municipal employment and for jobs with the public works service. Whereas emigration to Papeete to find work was once an option, increasing unemployment there, as well as the high cost of living, has discouraged young people from taking this course. Indeed, the recent wave of return migration to Tubuai from Papeete suggests that islanders believe that Tubuai may now offer, relatively speaking, more opportunities than Papeete.

Potato cultivation is one of those opportunities. Like women and return migrant families, young people have land, but no capital. But they do not need money or equipment to plant potatoes.

Middle- and High-Income Families

While these various factors motivated particular segments of the population to move into potato cultivation, one wonders why many relatively wealthy families—middle- and high-income earners—also cultivated potatoes (and also on a small scale). These families cultivated potatoes as a supplement to income—there was never enough money for islanders' rapidly expanding consumption agendas—and because potatoes had become a prestige food. French fries and potato salad had replaced other feast foods on important occasions and were a regular part of islanders' diets by the late 1980s. Because islanders are required to sell their entire harvest to the SDAP, the only way to have potatoes to eat is to grow them (and sell only part of them to the SDAP). By the late 1980s, many middle- and high-income families had come to think of potato cultivation as a three-month, seasonal "hobby" through which they acquired some extra income as well as potatoes for family meals.

One well-to-do young Tubuai woman, for example, started to plant potatoes in 1987. Her husband of several years had a well-paid (skilled) job with the public works service and they were in the high-income bracket on the island (earning about $24,000 a year). As this woman's parents had

had only daughters, she had worked extensively with her father (and mother) in their gardens while she was growing up. In 1987, she planted 750 kg of seed potatoes and produced a record harvest; she made $6,000 after expenses.

She and her husband decided to use the money to buy cement to lay the foundation for a large new Western-style house. When I returned to Tubuai in 1991, the house was finished and furnished, costing altogether almost $90,000. Although a bank loan paid for most of the construction, she continued planting potatoes each year, and her earnings helped cover the growing family's expenses and loan payments. Like most island families, this young couple had no savings. Every increase in income was immediately expended on new consumer purchases.

▲ Capitalist Development and the Peasant Mode of Production

On Tubuai, islanders' widespread involvement in a capital-intensive development program (and in capitalist markets in general) did not promote a transformation to capitalist relations of production. The complex interaction of both internal and external factors had discouraged large-scale potato cultivation and the concentration of land and wealth by a small group of "capitalist" farmers. Instead, potato cultivation had been incorporated into the mixed, small-scale pattern of household commodity production—a central feature of the peasant mode of production. Diverse factors had encouraged various segments of the population to undertake cultivation, but only on a risk-minimizing small scale. Small-scale cultivation also proved to be highly compatible with the system of familial land ownership and the household organization of labor. One must also conclude that unlike many development projects, the Tubuai potato project was truly benefiting the majority of the island population.

The Tubuai case and others from the Third World suggest that the peasant mode of production is a viable and resilient noncapitalist form that apparently thrives within encompassing capitalist economies. Indeed, Smith (1984) has argued that the commoditization of rural economies need not lead to the replication of capitalist class structures under certain conditions. She proposes that where familial commodity production can successfully compete with larger capitalist enterprises (because of price levels, the organization of production, economies of scale, and so on), and where subsistence production subsidizes the costs of market production, the peasant mode of production (commodity-producing peasant households) may prevail as the dominant mode of production.

On Tubuai, household production of potatoes can compete with other producers (from other nations) precisely because it does not have to compete.

Tubuai production is heavily subsidized to make it economically feasible for both producers and buyers; moreover, all imports of potatoes are halted when Tubuai potatoes are on the market. In other words, government policies have ensured that Tubuai potatoes will be produced and sold, even though less expensive imports are available on the world market.

Moreover, household production of commodities is directly subsidized by government transfer payments, including high salaries, family allocations, pensions, and various agricultural subsidies and aids. Households' ongoing subsistence production also serves as a subsidy to the high costs of commodity production.

Equally important in the perpetuation of the peasant mode of production on Tubuai is that most small cultivators could not have made the transition to large-scale commercial farming (even if this were economically attractive) because of the organization of household production (access to labor, etc.) and because of joint familial ownership of land. At the present time and under the present conditions, household-based commodity production meets the needs of the bulk of the island population quite well.

Thus, there are no forces at work internally on Tubuai promoting changes in the present organization of production, including land tenure, that might lead toward the local replication of capitalist relations of production. Instead, there are internal forces promoting the viability of the peasant mode of production: the drive of relatively economically marginal segments of the population—women, return migrants, and low-income families—to participate in commodity production on a small scale and in a household-based context.

In light of the apparent viability of the peasant mode of production, Smith (1984) suggests that the replication of capitalist relations of production in non-Western communities requires state intervention (as in England's enclosure movement). Such intervention is required to disrupt noncapitalist relations of production already in place, separate segments of the population from the means of production (creating land-owning and proletarian classes), and promote the growth of capitalist enterprise. On Tubuai, such state intervention could take the form of land tenure reform leading to the individualization of titles (private property).

Such intervention is unlikely to occur, however. The only reason for the French/territorial government to intervene would be if it believed that if farmers owned land individually, Tubuai could produce more potatoes (or vegetables) and thus make a greater contribution to the regional economy. Presumably, individual titles would allow large-scale farmers to concentrate control over parcels and expand production. But because of local conditions, individual titles would not promote increased production of potatoes and even if they did, Papeete markets could not absorb the increase.

For the many reasons that have been discussed, the commodity-producing peasant household is likely to remain the stable mode of production on Tubuai well into the future. It suggests that islanders can be major participants in capitalist markets without simultaneously participating in capitalist relations of production.[2]

▲ Notes

1. Between 1981 and 1987, approximately ninety-five new households came into existence: thirty-six were formed by return migrant families and fifty-nine by adult offspring setting up their own independent households. During this time, a few households had been disbanded as a result of emigration or death. Of the approximately 300 households in 1987, 282 were identified and included in an islandwide socioeconomic census.

2. Margaret Rodman (1993) describes a similar case for Vanuatu islanders.

▲ 8
Women and Development in Contemporary Rural Tahitian Society

In her classic study of women and development, Boserup (1970) argued that if women in typically male-dominated societies were able to achieve a greater role in new and typically male-controlled market activities (in "development"), their subordinate status in society would improve, becoming more equal to that of men. Women would not only be participating in the market economy, but also would presumably be playing a significantly greater role in economic decisionmaking, as well as in the control of products and disposition of earnings. Adopting this perspective, some scholars have proposed that programs be planned specifically for rural women to play a greater role in the development process.

Although Tubuai women's participation in development was neither planned nor anticipated, they have nevertheless assumed an important role in it, particularly in potato production and export. While many island women are now cultivating their own fields of potatoes and controlling the income, a few others hold wage jobs or market craft items.

Islanders are well aware that an important transformation has taken place in women's economic roles. This was made clear by the statements of a Tubuai man, statements that reveal a great deal about prevalent attitudes concerning the situation of contemporary women. In describing how women's lives had changed in the last twenty years, he said that they were now helping to *nourrir la famille* (feed and provide for the family—the male role); they were growing potatoes, holding jobs, and earning money other ways. And he went on the say that women's lives had only become harder as a result.

This informant's views corroborate the conclusion drawn in the earlier analysis of Tahitian peasant women's position: In commodity-producing households, women's many domestic/reproductive activities are not considered to be contributions to provisioning the family (as men's cash-earning activities are). But when women earn money, they too are "nourishing the family." This informant is also suggesting that women's lives had only become more difficult. Their situation had not improved as Boserup's (1970) analysis suggested it would.

▲ Women and New Economic Opportunities

With the exception of the recent potato project, women have been able to participate in only a limited way in the new economic opportunities introduced to the island. Of the approximately 194 jobs available today, only fifty-two (27 percent) are held by women. Most of these positions are for primary schoolteachers, cooks, secretaries, and cleaning personnel—jobs for which women are considered to be well-suited because they resemble women's activities in the domestic sphere (including working with children). In about thirty to thirty-five households, or in 10 percent of all households (N=300), women's salaries are the major source of income.

Women's participation in new kinds of commodity production (with the exception of potatoes and crafts) has also been limited, usually to labor contributions. For decades, women have participated in commodity production as helpers, while men controlled both production and income.

Today, many Tubuai women pursue their own small, independent, cash-earning activities, the most important of which was craft production until the potato project was introduced. Women produced and sold pandanus crafts, although due to the limited market for such items, craft production has never brought in much money. Although most island women belong to a craft association, only a few regularly sell their mats, hats, or quilts. About fifteen women earn an average of $100–$150 a month, and another five or six earn as much as $300–$400 a month. In some cases, particularly low-income households, this income may be a significant part of total family income.

Today, potato cultivation is the major cash-earning activity of island women. Whereas in 1983 only 20 percent of all potato farmers were women, in 1990 they were 43 percent of all planters (108 women and 143 men; see Table 8.1).[1] Moreover, the rate of increase in the numbers of new female farmers has been higher every year than the rate of increase in new male farmers. Most astoundingly, between 1987 and 1990, the number of male farmers actually declined by 23 percent, while the number of female farmers continued to increase, although at a slower rate than previously (by 16 percent; see Table 8.1).

▲ Women, Potatoes, and Subordination in the Household

The First Women Potato Cultivators

In 1980, four women signed up to plant potatoes in their own names with the agricultural service; by 1981 there were eight women planters. In many

Table 8.1 Tubuai Potato Cultivation by Gender, 1980–1991

						Average Cultivation Scale (kg/planted)	
		Number of Planters		% Increase	% Increase		
Year	Males	Females	Total	Males	Females	Males	Females
1980	37	4	41			1,780	625
1981	39	8	47	+5	+100	2,750	1,200
1983	82	20	102			1,300	770
1984	102	33	135	+48	+65	1,210	869
1985	125	47	172	+22	+42	1,030	766
1986	152	65	217	+21	+38	1,070	810
1987	186	93	279	+22	+43	1,260	870
1990	143	108	251	–23	+16	1,200	860

Notes: Information was provided by the Service de l'Économie Rurale, Tubuai, and by the Société de Développement d'Agriculture et de la Pêche, Tubuai; information for missing years is not available. Because information for 1982 is not available, the rate of increase in numbers of planters for 1983 was not calculated.

regards, these women were considered to be anomalies by the agricultural service and by the population at large. Although women were not specifically excluded from the project, no one had ever thought that they would sign on as potato cultivators. As mentioned earlier, men are considered to be the farmers, women playing only secondary roles in agriculture.

Most of these first women planters were older and came from what could be considered socially marginal households. Of the eight, five were in their mid-to-late fifties; the other three were in their early twenties. The five older women were relatively free of childcare responsibilities; only one of the three young women was married, and she was married to an elderly man. Only two of the married women's husbands brought in a regular income, one from a job and the other from vegetable cultivation. The employed husband, however, was a well-known drunk who squandered much of his income, while the vegetable cultivator was prone to erratic episodes of violence; in a rare incident in 1987, he was shot by his neighbor in a dispute. The incomes of the families of all eight women cultivators were in the lowest income bracket on the island. Their decision to plant potatoes was undoubtedly motivated by their need for money. Moreover, by virtue of either their age or marital status, most of these women were relatively free of male control.

In a study of a rural Oaxaca community, Browner (1986) identified similar characteristics among a small group of female innovators. These women were involved in community action to support new social programs, including a health clinic. The women who fought conservative male leadership opposed to the clinic were relatively free of male control either because they were not married or their husbands were migrant laborers. In addition, these women all played a major role in the economic support of their families. Browner (1986:102) notes that these characteristics "afforded [women] sufficient autonomy to act in their own interests as they perceived them."

In Tahitian communities, age and/or social marginality would also have contributed to the early women planters' ability to innovate. These characteristics would have meant that the early planters were relatively less sensitive to *ha'ama*, social embarrassment or shame caused by inappropriate (or inadequate) behavior in front of other people (in public) (see Levy 1973). Tahitians avoid *ha'ama* assiduously, and it is precisely in unfamiliar situations like potato cultivation that one is most at risk of public embarrassment.

The first women planters were not only unfamiliar with this male-oriented development project, but also they could not have known how the community would respond to them. In addition, if they failed, they would be doing so in a very public way. Both age and a certain social marginality would have diminished concerns these women might have had about what others in the community would think of them.

Thus, although women's independent potato cultivation was not viewed negatively by the community, the first women planters were not particularly admired role models for the large numbers of women who would later join the project. Nevertheless, these first planters did break down some of the perceived barriers for other women. It not only became clear that women would not be criticized for acting inappropriately, but that women could be a success at potato cultivation. In the following years, women started to join the project in large numbers.

The Characteristics of Women Planters and Their Households

Women's participation in the program has grown so quickly that by the late 1980s the contingent of women planters was a large and highly diverse group. Women planters today are of all ages and marital statuses (see Table 8.2) and come from households of all socioeconomic types (income levels and occupations; see Table 8.3). The typical female planter, however, is a married woman between the ages of 20 and 50 who has small or teenage children; this profile fits about 80 percent of all women cultivators. The other 20 percent are nonmarried, female household heads (widowed, separated, or divorced) who are supporting their families.

There are no major socioeconomic characteristics that distinguish the households of male and female cultivators, including income or primary economic occupation (see Table 8.3). Nor is there any statistically significant difference in female and male cultivators' households in family structure, household size, or in the developmental cycle of the family (see Tables 8.4 and 8.5). Young families with small children produce slightly fewer female

Tubuai women potato farmers cutting seed potatoes into sections in preparation for planting (photo: Lockwood).

planters, and the number of female planters (relative to males) increases as families mature.

Although many employed men also cultivate potatoes (42 percent of all males employed), only 15 percent of all employed females cultivate. It appears that while men can combine a job with potato farming, women are less able to combine a job, domestic responsibilities, and potato farming.

In households where men are employed (M2 and H2 households, see Table 8.3), their wives have a greater than expected rate of potato cultivation.

Table 8.2 Women Potato Cultivators: Age and Marital Status, 1987 (N=85)

Age	Number	%	Marital Status	Number	%
18–30 years	24	28	Married	60	71
31–40 years	27	32	Single	9	11
41–50 years	15	18	Separated	7	8
51 and older	19	22	Widowed	9	10
Total	85	100		85	100

Table 8.3 Distribution of Households of Male and Female Potato Cultivators by Income/Occupation

Income/ Occupation	Female Cultivators' Households	Male Cultivators' Households	No Potatoes	Total
Low income (L) Subsistence	18	23	5	46
Low/middle income (L/M) Retired	13	10	35	58
Middle income (MI) Marketer	3	18	6	27
Middle income (M2) Employed	25	33	14	72
High income (H0) Employed	9	13	13	35
(H1) Dual employment	4	5	16	25
(H2) Employment/markets	5	5	2	12
(H3) Exports/markets	3	5	1	9
Total	80	112	92	284
% of all Households	28%	39%	32%	100%

Note: Female cultivators' households may also include a male cultivator.

Table 8.4 Family Structure and Size of Households of Female and Male Potato Cultivators, 1987 (N=191)

	Family Structure				Household Size		
	Nuclear	Extended	Composite	1–3	4–6	7–9	10–14
Households of female cultivators	55	11	14	9	38	25	8
Households of male cultivators	84	14	13	20	55	23	13
Total	139	25	27	29	93	48	21

Family structure: Chi-square=1.45; p=.4833.
Household size: Chi-square=3.162; p=.3058.

Table 8.5 Households of Male and Female Potato Cultivators: Stage in the
Developmental Cycle of the Family, 1987 (N=191)

Stage in the Family Cycle	Households of Female Cultivators	Households of Male Cultivators	Total
A	22	42	64
B	33	40	73
C	10	16	26
Composite households	15	13	28
Total	80	111	191

Notes: Female cultivators' households may also include a male cultivator.
Chi-square=3.50; p=.3195.
A=Household heads are less than 40 years of age and still reproductively active; household includes small children.
B=Household heads are middle-aged (40–60 years); children are teenagers; household may include small adopted grandchildren and/or adult children's young spouses.
C=Household heads are over 60 years of age; household may include small adopted children and/or adult children with their families.

In the households where males are not employed but are major commodity producers (M1 and H3 households), women have a lower than expected rate of cultivation. These patterns suggest that in the households where males are major producers, a wife's cultivation would probably compete with her husband's cultivation for familial land and labor. As a result, in these market-oriented households, women may have the fewest opportunities for independent economic activity and therefore the least economic autonomy. Where men are employed and thus less involved in agriculture and commodity production, women can more readily make use of familial resources in their own economic pursuits.

Women Cultivators and Class?

In many developing communities, "economic change is likely to affect women of different classes differently depending on their access/control of capital (money) and other resources" (Stoler 1977:75). In the Javanese example that Stoler describes, upper-class women with access to capital have been able to parlay that capital into social power. Women with no capital have had a much different experience with capitalism. Class membership is thus an important factor shaping how women participate in capitalism.

But as noted previously, although there are rapidly growing wealth differences between island households, this has not been associated with the emergence of capitalist class relations. All households retain control of the means of production—land—and no true proletariat (group separated from the means of production and thus forced to sell its labor) exists. All women (like all men) have access to familial land, and all women can obtain the capital needed to cultivate through the government's loan system. Thus, women's (or anyone's else) participation in potato cultivation is not influenced by class-related differential control of capital or land.

It is interesting, however, as noted above, that in the households most heavily involved in capitalist markets, of those who specialize in commodity production and export, women (wives) are less likely to become independent potato cultivators. One might assume that in these most market-oriented households, women might be more likely to undertake their own market production. But this is not the case.

Women, Labor, and Scale of Cultivation

Tubuai women's participation in the potato project is directly facilitated by the many aids and subsidies provided by the government, particularly the loans that cover incurred costs prior to harvest. Women's lack of capital would otherwise create a major barrier to their potato cultivation. Although women are not hampered by lack of capital, they are hampered by reduced access to labor.

Most of a woman's time is consumed by tasks associated with the maintenance of the household, childcare, and food preparation, as well as by her work in her husband's fields. While there is flexibility in the sexual division of labor, one never sees men wash or sew clothes, dress small children for school, sweep the house, or weave floor mats. Although men cook, they do little other housework. Thus, unless a woman has a teenage daughter to help her with her domestic work, she must continue to do it in addition to whatever other activities she takes on. Women potato planters can and do call on the labor of husbands and children to help in their fields, but because most men either have jobs or cultivate their own fields and most children are in school, a woman is not likely to receive a great deal of help.

Consequently, most women cultivate on a significantly smaller scale than men. In 1990, women planted approximately 860 kg of seed potatoes on average, while men planted about 1,200 kg (see Table 8.1). Scale of planting is the only major difference in the cultivation strategies of male and female planters.

It should be mentioned that most island women avoid entering gardens and fields (or touching plants) during their menstrual periods, although this practice does not appear to limit their cultivation in any way. Islanders believe that menstrual blood causes plants to wilt and die. Although one cannot say for sure, this may be linked to centuries-old beliefs concerning the supposed danger/contaminating effects (and power) of women's biological processes (see Chapter 3). Tubuai women are careful to dispose of used rags or napkins by either burning or burying them. Because the maintenance demands of potato fields—occasional weeding and applications of fertilizers and insecticides—are sporadic as opposed to constant, a woman's absence from her fields for a brief number of days is not a problem. Similarly, the scheduling of planting, harvesting, and mounding young plants is relatively flexible.

Women Planters' Motives and Goals

As mentioned above, women potato planters are largely of two types: married women and nonmarried female household heads (see Table 8.6). The vast majority of the nonmarried women's households, 81 percent, are in the low-income range and potatoes are frequently the major source of income. In these cases, women cultivate potatoes out of economic necessity.

Table 8.6 Female Potato Cultivators' Marital Status and Household Incomes/ Occupations, 1987

Household Economic Code[a]	Married[b]	Single Female Household Heads	Total
L	13	8	21
LM	12	5	17
M1	5	0	5
M2	21	3	24
H0	6	0	6
H1	3	0	3
H2	6	0	6
H3	3	0	3
Total	69	16	85

[a]See Table 8.3 for explanation of code.
[b]This category includes nine cultivators who are single daughters or granddaughters of the household; there are actually sixty married women in this category.

The situation of married women (and daughters in families) is significantly different, however, because many of these women come from middle- and high-income households (see Table 8.6). In interviews, women planters frequently cited as major considerations in their decision to cultivate a desire to have their own money (which they could spend as they please) and a desire to be less financially dependent on husbands. Some women potato planters are motivated by the desire to make specific consumer purchases, such as a sewing or washing machine. Others simply want to earn money for the household, children, and themselves.

Most married women described their decision to plant potatoes as one they had made independently and as an act of personal volition. Unlike in some societies where wives are considered to be extensions of their husbands and rarely act independently, in Tahitian society married couples view themselves as two independent individuals who have agreed to cooperate in some areas to form a household/family. And wives strive to act independently when they have the wherewithal (financial, etc.) to do so.

Islanders say that money and divergent consumption priorities are frequently causes of marital discord, and both men and women complain about how their spouses spend money. Women frequently disapprove when their husbands buy large quantities of beer or other kinds of liquor (women rarely drink) or cigarettes; both are expensive. Men disapprove of women's desire for imported Western-style dresses and other accoutrements. For the most part, both men and women consider it the wife's/mother's role to purchase necessities for the household such as food and clothing. But men may not agree with a wife who wants to make specific purchases, and wives are frequently resentful of their husbands' control of cash income.

These differences should not be taken to mean that Tahitian marriages are any more fragile (or disharmonious) than marriages elsewhere. They only mean that in this consumer-oriented and rapidly Westernizing community, money can quickly become a point of contention in some households.

Wage earners used to receive their pay in cash on payday, and islanders say that men would typically give a portion to wives, who bought the family's basic necessities. But in the last ten years, government agencies have started depositing salary checks directly into a wage earner's bank account. Similarly, potato earnings are deposited directly into the farmer's SOCREDO account. This gives the person whose name is on the account control over the money it holds, and other family members—most often wives—do not have access to it. Thus, women may have less access to familial cash income than ever before.

Even though a woman potato cultivator's goal is to have her own money to spend as she wishes, this does not mean that a husband will refuse to help or cooperate with her. Many husbands do work in their wives' fields when they are able, and they are not openly resentful of her income. There are a few cases, however, where a woman's potato cultivation is a direct reflection of serious marital discord and perhaps open conflict. The most obvious cases are when both a husband and wife cultivate their own independent fields during the same season. In these cases there is likely to be significantly less cooperation between spouses. In 1987, this was the situation in eighteen households, or for 20 percent of all women planters.

Women's Limited Visions and "Nonserious" Status

For the most part, women have limited visions of what they can accomplish and how much they can earn planting potatoes. The purchase of a sewing machine is more than an adequate accomplishment for one season (see also Langevin 1990:129). Moreover, even after several years of successful cultivation, women's aspirations remain limited. On the one hand, this reflects the real constraints that affect how much time women can devote to cultivation. On the other hand, it reflects many women's belief that males are the real provisioners in the family and that women should rightfully play a secondary role and "tend to the householdwork."

Since most women do cultivate potatoes on a small scale and their goal is to generate a small supplement to household income, the agricultural service tends to define them as "nonserious" planters. The agricultural service also defines most higher-income, small-scale male planters the same way. In the past several years, as the number of planters and areas to be cultivated have grown, the service has found its resources strained to the limit. In particular, it has become harder and harder to give all farmers access to the few tractors and other equipment the service operates. Officials hint that if program cutbacks must be made (due to marketing or other problems), such small-scale, "nonserious" planters may be affected first.

Domestic Power: Potato Cultivation and Women's Position in the Household

In an earlier chapter, I discussed the direct relationship between male control of most cash income and male authority/decisionmaking prerogatives in the Tahitian commodity-producing household. The question immediately arises as to how women's increasing assumption of the male role of provisioner and women's greater personal control of cash income will affect the prevailing patterns of gender stratification in the Tahitian household. For the reasons discussed below, it appears that the changes in women's economic roles will have little impact.

Through potato cultivation, Tubuai women have indeed been able to achieve some personal financial autonomy, and this is highly valued by them. But island women have always earned small amounts of money from sales of their crafts and from family allocations, and this has not posed a threat to established patterns of male authority/decisionmaking in the household. In the average Tubuai household—income about $12,000 a year—women's potato earnings ($1,000 per season) constitute only 8 percent of total income. It is only in situations where a woman is the major provider in the family and her earnings are more than just a supplement to family income that male authority in the rural Tahitian household becomes open to challenge. Finney (1973:83) recognized this in his early study of Tahitian society (see Chapter 3), and it remains true today.

Women are the major providers in only a small number of households, about 10–15 percent of all households. These households include some in which the wife is employed and her husband is neither employed nor produces significant quantities of marketable commodities. They also include low-income households (16 percent of all island households) where the money a woman brings in from potato farming, in conjunction with her family allocations, constitutes the bulk of family income. In all other cases, men bring in the majority of family earnings.

It is unlikely, for the many reasons discussed above, that island women would be able to expand their potato cultivation and to earn larger incomes, thereby challenging male financial control. Further, there is no evidence of forces at work that might alter the prevailing division of labor or patterns of income earning.

To achieve the greater financial autonomy and ability to help provision the family, which many rural Tahitian women value, they must work harder. Women must combine potato farming with their other domestic responsibilities. Although that labor investment and the money it brings into the family directly promotes the financial well-being of the household, it does not simultaneously enable a woman to participate as an equal in household decisionmaking with male heads of households, or to have a greater say in how the family's money is expended. Thus, greater income earning and financial autonomy does not mean greater domestic power for women (see Kung 1976 for a similar case). Even so, women have assessed the relative costs and benefits of potato cultivation and have clearly made the choice to work harder.

▲ Women, Prestige, and Power in Rural Communities

Women's Social Status and Prestige

Women's changing roles raise questions about the kinds of activities for which women are valued and accorded social prestige. In Tahitian society, a "good" woman is one who successfully and diligently performs her domestic/reproductive tasks, her "natural" domain. Women gain prestige in the community predominantly through motherhood (by having and nurturing numerous children) and by keeping well-maintained houses, typically surrounded by much-admired gardens of colorful flowers and shrubs. Women who cannot have children usually adopt them from others, achieving the prestige of motherhood this way. A married woman who has no child and does not adopt one, or a woman whose child arrives for Sunday services in torn or dirty clothing, is the target of severe gossip and criticism.

Women can also gain prestige in the community through their hard work and participation in church activities. Women's church groups typically organize the food sales and other activities through which churches make money. Women who are good organizers and who devote their time and effort to church affairs may be rewarded by being elected to head their women's church group. In addition to organizing community events to make money, women's church groups also convene socially to work on large pandanus floor mats or to study the Bible.

Women who produce superior craft items (for home or sale), a traditional female activity, also gain prestige in the community. During the July 14 (Bastille Day) festival, women's craft associations hold competitions and women are awarded prizes for the most beautiful items.

But increasingly, women, like men, are gaining prestige for the work they do to bring in money. Cash is always scarce. Being a hard worker and helping the family to prosper economically, whether through craft production, potato cultivation, or wage work, is highly valued. And women, like men, can also gain prestige from their material possessions. Women envy other women who live in new, Western-style houses, who wear ready-made Western-style clothes, and who possess items such as washing and sewing machines.

Women and Power in the Community

While women gain prestige and are esteemed for their predominantly domestic-related roles and activities, none hold positions of power or authority in the community. Indeed, when one looks at where the real power lies in rural Tahitian society, one see that it is in domains completely dominated by men. As noted previously, power in the community, or the ability to shape island affairs and public policies and to make decisions critical to the well-being of the community, is derived from control of the government resources that sustain island society at its presently high standard of living. Thus, the island's administration, the elected mayor and island council, and the heads of various government agencies—all men—wield a great deal of power. The only positions women hold in administration are secretarial.

Other important loci of power in the community are the branches of Papeete political parties and the agricultural cooperative. These too are run and dominated by men. Church leaders—all men—also wield important kinds of social (and moral) power, if not direct economic or political power.

Although men control all of these power domains, that does not mean that women are absent from them. Unfortunately, some scholars who have studied Tahitian society have tended to assume that because women were active (present) in community affairs they also played powerful roles there. Levy (1973:198) notes, for example:

> Since pre-Christian times the political, social, and household power of
> women has been, compared with many other societies, close to the power
> and authority of men, and this situation still obtains. Although there are
> some pieties about women properly deferring to men, in action and

assumptions about "how things really are" there is little of this and women are actively involved not only in household management but in most village affairs.

Women are indeed active in community affairs. There are just as many women as men who attend the meetings of the agricultural cooperative and the town meetings convened when territorial officials visit the island. Moreover, some women are just as vocal as men in expressing their opinions about co-op affairs, the island's budget, or government mismanagement. But it is only through the expression of her views that a woman might hope to influence the perspectives of the male leaders who actually determine public policy. The male heads of the commune, co-op, and government agencies make the critical decisions that affect the community.

In an indirect (and male-biased) way, Levy (1973:502) goes on to acknowledge women's absence from leadership roles and lack of real power in Tahitian communities:

Women's lives in Piri and Roto [Tahitian villages] seem culturally simpler than men's lives. Girls usually stay close to the household, and their adult role is in many ways a continuation of their childhood and adolescent life. Boys have more discontinuities. They break out of childhood into the *taure'are'a* [adolescent] life. . . . They must eventually play household and village roles which are more different from their childhood roles than is the case for women.

He also notes: "Men are in the forefront of village political activity, with the women as an interested and vocal background" (Levy 1973:233).

To a certain extent, women's time-consuming domestic and reproductive responsibilities—those activities for which they are socially valued—leave them little time to participate in activities that might give them a more prominent public profile. For example, although many women are now participating in the potato project, the other demands on their time and labor mean that most do so only on a small scale. Consequently, as noted above, most women are not considered by agricultural officials or co-op leaders to be "serious" farmers. Thus, it is not surprising that even though almost half of the agricultural co-op's members are women, there were no female officers or female candidates in the election for co-op officers that took place in 1987.

In general, both men and women feel that men should appropriately hold important community and church offices and that men should be the heads of their families. Although women speak up about community matters when they have a chance and strive to have their own money, both male and female Tahitians are well imbued with the Western/Christian ideology that says that women will follow men, not lead, in most of life's endeavors.

▲ Women, Land, and Power

While one can argue that the most strategic resource at this time in Tubuai's development is cash income (and it is controlled mostly by men), it is important to note that the major means of production—land—is in part owned by women. And as discussed earlier, women do achieve some clout in the household by virtue of their ownership of land. This is particularly true if the family resides on and cultivates a woman's familial land. In these cases, a wife will have a greater say in how land is used. However, because her husband is considered to be the owner of the gardens and fields he plants on the land, a wife will not necessarily have control of the cash earnings from those gardens. And because land is not absolutely scarce, nor is it considered by most islanders to be a market commodity, women's ownership of land is at present relatively insignificant to any consideration of women's relative power in the household and community.

If for whatever reason such a market in land did develop, women would find themselves in the position of owning the most strategic resource on the island. Undoubtedly the development of a market in land would be associated with the full-scale replication of capitalist relations of production on the island. In this case, women who owned land would find themselves potentially in the position of capitalist (as opposed to labor).

Since political and economic power in all capitalist systems, whether in the community or the household, is ultimately linked to differential control of the means of production, ownership of land may, in the future, become a source of power for rural Tahitian women. Barnes (1990) has noted, for example, that among the urban Yoruba of southwest Nigeria, women who own property (mostly houses) and control capital possess the same kinds of independence, authority, and power as males. She goes on to say that "the power that both women and men acquire in the domestic context, if they own and thereby control that context, acts as a natural bridge to the public realm" (Barnes 1990:276). If the Tahitian peasant mode of production were ever to give way to a full penetration of capitalist relations, it is conceivable that female landowners' status in both the household and community might become more equal to that of males.

It is difficult, however, to predict exactly how land use and ownership patterns would be affected if collective holdings were divided and land became private property. Such divisions would cause extreme land fragmentation. It is likely that individuals' tiny portions would be too small for potato cultivation (even on a small scale) and too small for effective use of the agricultural service's tractor and bulldozer. Farmers would probably try to (and need to) amass a number of holdings (probably belonging to their kin). It is likely that the many nonresident landowners, as well as resident wage earners (and others only minimally involved in agricultural commodity production), would sell their tiny portions to those seeking more land.

Because women have little access to capital, it is unlikely that they would be able to buy land. Men, on the other hand, especially those who specialize in commodity production, would be in a position to buy up land. Thus, if land became private property, the dual phenomena of fragmentation in conjunction with male attempts to concentrate holdings might cause women—the "nonserious" farmers—to lose the land they own. If women lost their land, they would also lose any potential increase in status or power the status of landowner might have brought them.

▲ Rural Tahitian Women and Capitalism

The possibility that a greater penetration of capitalist relations of production might actually improve rural Tahitian women's position and endow them with greater economic and political power raises a number of important questions about how capitalism specifically impinges upon women's lives. At present, a substantial body of literature supports the contention that as capitalism penetrates developing communities, women's position deteriorates (Fernandez-Kelly 1981; Caulfield 1981; Bossen 1984). This literature argues that even though women may have played important roles in production and controlled resources in the precapitalist "traditional" society, following market integration men typically dominate new market-related activities and become defined as the "owners" (usually within introduced systems of private property) of capital (see Sexton 1993, Afonja 1981 for examples). Women become financially dependent on and economically subordinate to men. Consequently, they become their political subordinates and are denied an active role in household and community decisionmaking.

But in the rural Tahitian case, land did not become defined as owned by men. The French created a legal system of bilateral ownership, and islanders took that system and made it into one that fit their needs and worldview. They did this by refashioning it into a system of collective, joint (nonindividual) bilateral inheritance by all of one's heirs.

It is interesting to note that Hawaiian women also retained ownership of land following the massive, colonial-era changes that took place in their society. Linnekin (1990) describes how even though Hawaiian women were "devalued by the dominant [Western] ideology" in a way very similar to the devaluation of Tahitian women, their local and domestic importance was enhanced because they were landowners. Moreover, because Hawaiian men were frequently absent (migration, jobs, and so on), women often became the major household authorities. Thus, Linnekin (1990) has identified a real discrepancy between the ideological denigration of Hawaiian women and their actual position of relative power in Hawaiian households and communities.

Both the Tahitian and Hawaiian cases, as well as the Yoruba case, lead one to question the prevailing view among development scholars that capitalism automatically leads to the disenfranchisement of women in developing non-Western communities. In those cases where women, for whatever reason, retain control over land or other critical means of production, they can (in theory) potentially occupy the same economically and politically powerful niches that men occupy.

According to Barnes's (1990) analysis, it appears that Yoruba women do occupy those niches. But the cases of Hawaiian and Tahitian women are complicated by the strong Christian church–backed ideology that defines women as subordinate to men. They are also complicated by the prevailing general Western/capitalist ideology that denigrates women's domestic and reproductive contributions and defines their capabilities as generally inferior to those of men. One would expect that in the Tahitian case, if land does become a market commodity and women garner greater economic clout as a result, the prevailing ideology would change to reflect "reality." This, however, remains an area for future research.

Clearly, the relationship between capitalism and women's position in society is a complex one. It is by looking at specific cases like the Tahitians, Hawaiians, and Yorubas that one can gain an appreciation of the great diversity of ways in which women have been affected by capitalist development and by the integration of their communities into the world system.

▲ Note

1. Some of these data were first presented in Lockwood (1989).

▲ 9
Conclusions: Scenarios for the Future

Looking at the structure of the world system today, one must conclude that Tahitians, and most other Pacific islanders, occupy a highly marginal position in that system. Like many other remote areas of the Third World, they have few resources of interest to offer in the international marketplace, except their human resources in the form of labor. Extensive out-migration from many Pacific islands societies to Western metropolitan centers—and the islands' subsequent depopulation and underdevelopment—reflects this situation.

Unlike many other island societies, the Tahitian islands of French Polynesia have escaped this fate and instead are actively being "developed" under the auspices of the financially benevolent French welfare state. In projecting what the future may be like for Tahitian men and women, it is important to recognize that much of what Tahitian society is today (and certainly what it has in a material sense) is the product of French engineering.

Although in their politically subordinate and economically dependent role, islanders have little control over French agendas, they have not adopted a passive and unquestioning stance to the external forces affecting their lives. Despite their dependency, islanders have agendas too, and within the framework of French welfare state colonialism and capitalist development, they pursue those agendas.

▲ The Peasant Mode of Production:
Maintaining Options and Security

It is clear that the peasant mode of production in rural Tahitian society, particularly the noncapitalist features of it (e.g., the land tenure system), are not on the list of French agendas, nor compatible with them. At the same time, one has to notice how well part capitalism works for a large number of rural Tahitians. Although many forces have interacted to perpetuate the peasant mode of production, one reason it remains viable today is that it represents islanders' agendas: It is in part their solution to the way in which they have been integrated into the regional and world capitalist economies.

The maintenance of similar socioeconomic forms in other Pacific islands societies has been described by a number of anthropologists. Rodman (1993), for example, has analyzed how Vanuatu islanders opt out of capitalism, periodically retiring from market production (copra and fish) to ensure their security through subsistence production and by maintaining extensive kin/social obligations. She argues that they do this because incentives promoting market production, particularly strong prices, are weak, and islanders have few other available cash-earning options.

Similarly, Petersen (1993) contends that Pohnpei islanders (Federated States of Micronesia, part of the former U.S. trust territory of Micronesia) actively work to minimize the impact of capitalism on their lives. He cites the example of the purposeful bankruptcies of trade store owners. Instead of selling merchandise to make profits, owners see it more to their advantage to give it away (through ceremonial redistribution) to attain social prestige within the traditional political economy. Petersen links such activities to Pohnpei islanders' desire for full political independence from the United States and to their desire for local self-sufficiency (security) and less dependence on the United States (salaries, transfer payments, and imports).

Both Rodman and Petersen interpret islanders' maintenance of noncapitalist forms as at least in part a rejection of capitalism, and in this, Tahitians differ from them. Even though rural Tahitians have avoided the commoditization of their land (shift to private property) and labor and chosen not to abandon subsistence production in favor of full-scale market production, they have definitely "thrown their lot in with the cash economy"—a phenomenon first noted by Finney (1973) in the 1960s. In contrast to other Pacific islanders, French welfare state colonialism has brought rural Tahitians unprecedented opportunities (by local, pan-Pacific, and Third World standards) to participate in capitalism as commodity producers and import consumers. Even at the cost of their neocolonial domination, most islanders—and particularly young people—would like more participation, not less. Rural Tahitians do not reject capitalism, and it is not possible to interpret their maintenance of the peasant mode of production as such.

Affluence, Security, and Land

On the other hand, despite their affluence, one of rural Tahitians' major agendas is security. In this they are surprisingly like other significantly less affluent, less market-oriented Pacific islanders. Even though the potato project has been a success, islanders' economic options within the fragile territorial economy have deteriorated over the last decade. At the present time, the future of Tubuai's green vegetable exports looks bleak because of repeatedly intractable marketing problems. Potato production has been capped at 1,200 tons, a quantity substantially less than what the growing number of potato farmers is capable of producing. Islanders' out-migration/find work in Papeete option has become less viable as both unemployment and the cost of living have increased in the city; high rates of return migration and outer-island population retention reflect this. And finally, while the number of jobs has not decreased on Tubuai, government employment opportunities are more or less finite. Thus, as the number of islanders looking for work steadily increases—young people, return migrants, and so on—jobs are becoming relatively scarcer.

On Tubuai, government employees are relatively economically secure, although commodity producers are not; for the latter, income levels have the potential of rising and falling unexpectedly. Moreover, islanders are aware that their options are becoming more constrained. In their present economic environment, their major goal is to maintain their standard of living at its current level. Thus, while other Pacific islanders are worried about being able to feed their families and buy a few imported luxuries, Tubuaians are worried about not losing the high level of consumption that is now so much a part of their lives.

In other words, security is relative. The more one has, the more one has to lose, and Tubuaians are well aware of how much they have. It also seems that the more one has, the more difficult it is to give any of it up or to contemplate returning to a lifestyle that was materially less affluent. Although quite elderly Tahitians might venerate the more traditional past on Tubuai, no one under the age of 60 does so. Islanders do not even possess a romanticized version of their own "traditional" past: They value what is modern and Western. Their commitment to (and aspirations of) achieving the Western lifestyle they see portrayed on television makes it difficult for them to consider living any other way (living with less). They would not even consider living like their grandparents did—a time when islanders claim life on the outer islands was primitive and *sauvage.*

Under the present economic conditions, access to land is critical to achieving at least a minimum acceptable standard of living on the island. It is interesting that both young people and return migrants have gained a new appreciation of the traditional land tenure system because it has ensured their access to land. Rights to land enable islanders to feed their families from subsistence gardens and to cultivate potatoes and green vegetables and make money. Considering the limited number of jobs (both on Tubuai and in Papeete), commercial agriculture is probably the most viable economic option for many segments of the population.

I believe that islanders are well aware of what has happened to land on the more modernized islands of the territory, including Tahiti, where it is private property. On these islands, families have sold land to acquire money and in so doing have forced themselves to enter the limited urban labor market. The best parcels have been alienated to developers of one sort or another. If land on Tubuai were to become private property and easily sold, islanders recognize that many local families would lose their control over land, and thus they would lose one of their economic options and the security it entails. I believe that this is why so few Tubuaians—with the exception of those who want to build new, permanent houses—favor land divisions and the individualization of land tenure.

Certainly, Tubuai women have benefited greatly from their access to land within the familial system. If they did not own or have access to land, they would be unable to cultivate potatoes, participate in development, and achieve the greater (if limited) financial autonomy they value. As noted earlier, it is possible that if land were privatized, many island women would lose their control (ownership) over land, and thus their options for achieving autonomy would be significantly curtailed.

Subsistence Production

Allocating some familial resources (land and labor) to subsistence production is another strategy for increasing islanders' options as well as their security. Islanders are proud of saying that no one on Tubuai need ever be poor, and in this they are not referring to their welfare payments. They are referring to the bounty of their land and lagoon. Imported foods are expensive, and even though cash may be scarce and economic misfortune might strike, islanders can ensure their ability to feed their families by cultivating relatively low-maintenance subsistence gardens.

Moreover, avoiding expenditures on imported foods also gives islanders more discretionary cash income (in good times) to expend on expensive manufactured items and luxuries. Thus, subsistence production allows islanders to participate more extensively as consumers in the international capitalist marketplace.

▲ The Future

Since it appears that French financial support of the territory and of its economic programs will continue, there is every reason to believe that in the near future few changes will take place in the territory and in the organization of rural Tahitian society. Islanders' demands for independence from France would severely disrupt this scenario, but such demands are unlikely. Islanders' commitment to their present standard of living—one of the "benefits" of affiliation with France—binds them to France in a way that virtually precludes separation.

Moreover, islanders do not perceive themselves as dependent or as colonials (see Lockwood 1993). Although they complain about French policies—particularly the nuclear testing and the high cost of living—they do not perceive their interests as being different from or in opposition to those of France. In addition, French relaxation of its cultural assimilationist policies and nominal encouragement of a revived Tahitian ethnic identity (language, and so on) has prevented ethnic issues from becoming political issues in the territory. For all of these reasons, it is difficult to identify forces that might fuel a future Tahitian nationalist or separatist movement.

Rural Tahitian Society

The process that is most likely to threaten the present lifestyle of rural islanders, as well as the viability of the peasant mode of production, is rural population growth. Since the number of government jobs on Tubuai is finite and there appears to be little potential for growth in commodity production and export, the island economy cannot support a continuously growing population, at least not at islanders' present standard of living.

If government salaries continue to increase but other economic options remain limited, the present gap between wage-earning families and others will become only more extreme. Even if agricultural commodity producers could acquire control over more land, the weak and fluctuating territorial and world markets for their produce would hamper increasing output. One can expect that competition for the best agricultural lands, and thus for a bigger slice of the limited export market, will increase. Such competition, and the growing number of familial disputes over land associated with it, could potentially bring about the individualization of land tenure so long avoided. This would effectively catalyze the local-level transition to capitalist relations of production.

There are many unknown variables that might enter this picture, however. French financial support and welfare payments might increase, maintaining islanders' standard of living despite a growing population and shrinking opportunities. Or France might devise new local-level development programs aimed at exploiting presently untouched territorial resources such as fish or various kinds of indigenous crops. Or France might facilitate and encourage the international migration of some of the territory's growing population; this has been one strategy utilized by the French state in its Caribbean island possessions.

While the future is difficult to predict, Tahitian society will undoubtedly continue to experience the fallout from its political relationship with France. And as France continues its efforts to develop a niche for the islands in the world system, Tahitian men's and women's lives will become more caught up in the machinations of international capitalism.

▲

Tahitian Terms

ari'i	aristocracy of chiefs and their families
fa'a'amu	informal adoption
faaapu	fields
fafa	steamed taro leaves in coconut sauce
fare ni'au	traditional-style Tahitian house
fenua feti'i	family land
feti'i	bilateral kindred
firifiri	Tahitian doughnut
ha'ama	social embarrassment/shame
ha'avare	falsehood
hei's	necklaces
mana	supernatural power
manahune	commoners
marae	sacred stone platform where rituals and sacrifices were performed
mutoi	local police
noa	the profane/secular
ni'au	coconut fiber
pareu	length of cloth wrapped around the waist
po'e	fruit pudding
popoi	mashed and fermented taro wrapped in banana leaves
pupu	cooperative work group
ra'atira	lesser chiefs and bureaucrats
ra'a/mo'a	the sacred
ra'au Tahiti	Tahitian medicine
ta'ata Tahiti	Tahitians
tapa	barkcloth
tapus	supernaturally proscribed behavior
tara	five francs
taure'are'a	the carefree, adolesent stage in the life cycle
tavana	chief/elected mayo
tifaifai	quilts
tupapa'u	ghosts
umu	earth oven

▲
References

Afonja, Simi
    1981 "Changing Modes of Production and the Sexual Division of Labor Among the Yoruba." *Signs* 7 (2): 299–313.

Aitken, R.
    1930 *Ethnology of Tubuai.* Bulletin no. 40. Honolulu: Bernice P. Bishop Museum.

Aldrich, R., and J. Connell
    1989 *France in World Politics.* London: Routledge.

Amin, Samir
    1976 *Unequal Development.* New York: Monthly Review Press.

Babadzan, Alan
    1982 *Naissance d'une Tradition: Changement Culturel et Syncrétisme Religieux aux Îles Australes (P.F.).* Travaux et Documents, no. 154. Paris: Office de la Recherche Scientifique et Technique d'Outre-Mer (ORSTOM).

Barnes, Sandra
    1990 "Women, Property and Power." In *Beyond the Second Sex,* P. Sanday and R. Goodenough, eds., pp. 253–280. Philadelphia: University of Pennsylvania Press.

Bellwood, Peter
    1987 *The Polynesians: Prehistory of an Island People.* London: Thames and Hudson.

Bertram, G.
    1986 "'Sustainable Development' in Pacific Micro-Economies." *World Development* 14 (7): 809–822.

Bertram, I. G., and R. F. Watters
    1985 "The MIRAB Economy of the South Pacific Microstates." *Pacific Viewpoint* 26: 497–519.

Blanchet, Gilles
    1984 *L'Économie de la Polynésie Française de 1960 à 1980.* Notes et Documents, no. 10. Papeete: Office de la Recherche Scientifique et Technique d'Outre-Mer (ORSTOM).

Borofsky, R., and A. Howard
    1989 "The Early Contact Period." In *Developments in Polynesian Ethnology,* A. Howard and R. Borofsky, eds., pp. 241–276. Honolulu: University of Hawaii Press.

Boserup, Ester
1970 *Women's Role in Economic Development*. London: George Allen and Unwin.
Bossen, Laurel
1975 "Women in Modernizing Societies." *American Ethnologist* 2 (4): 587–601.
1984 *The Redivision of Labor: Women and Economic Choice in Four Guatemalan Communities*. Albany: State University of New York Press.
Breeze, Richard
1981 "The Thorn in France's Rose." *Far Eastern Economic Review* 113 (September 11–17): 30–33.
Browner, Carol
1986 "Gender Roles and Social Change: A Mexican Case Study." *Ethnology* 25 (2): 89–106.
Buton, Nadine
1974 "Contribution à l'Étude de la Vie Rurale à Taahuahia de Tubuai (Archipel des Australes)." Master's Thesis, Université de Bordeaux, France.
Campbell, I. C.
1989 *A History of the Pacific Islands*. Berkeley: University of California Press.
Cancian, Frank
1972 *Change and Uncertainty in a Peasant Economy: The Maya Corn Farmers of Zinacantan*. Stanford: Stanford University Press.
1979 *The Innovator's Situation: Upper Middle Class Conservatism in Agricultural Communities*. Stanford: Stanford University Press.
Caulfield, Mina
1981 "Equality, Sex, and the Mode of Production." In *Social Inequality: Comparative and Developmental Approaches*, G. Berremen, ed., pp. 201–219. New York: Academic Press.
Charlton, Sue Ellen
1984 *Women in Third World Development*. Boulder: Westview Press.
Chesneaux, Jean
1986 "France in the Pacific: Global Approach or Respect for Regional Agendas?" *Bulletin of Concerned Asian Scholars* 18:73–80.
Connell, John
1980 "Remittances and Rural Development: Migration, Dependency, and Inequality in the South Pacific." Occasional Paper no. 22, Development Studies Centre, Australian National University, Canberra.
1984 "Modernity and Its Discontents: Migration and Social Change in the South Pacific." Paper presented at workshop, Consequences of International Migration. International Union for the Scientific Study of Population, Canberra.
1985 *Migration, Employment, and Development in the South Pacific*. Country Report no. 5, French Polynesia. Noumea: International Labour Organization, South Pacific Commission.
Cook, Jon
1976 "Subsistence Farmers and Fishermen of Tubuai." Ph.D. diss., University of Kansas.
Cook, Scott
1982 *Zapotec Stoneworkers: The Dynamics of Rural Simple Commodity Production in Modern Mexican Capitalism*. Washington, D.C.: University Press of America.
Crocombe, Ronald
1971a "Land Reform: Prospects for Prosperity." In *Land Tenure in the Pacific*. R. Crocombe, ed., pp. 375–400. Melbourne: Oxford University Press.

1971b "Overview: The Pattern of Change in Pacific Land Tenure." In *Land Tenure in the Pacific.* R. Crocombe, ed., pp. 1–24. Melbourne: Oxford University Press.

1987 *The South Pacific: An Introduction.* Auckland, New Zealand: Longman Paul.

Crocombe, R., and P. Hereniko, eds.
1985 *Tahiti: The Other Side.* Suva, Fiji: University of the South Pacific.

Danielsson, Bengt
1955 *Raroia: Happy Island of the South Seas.* Chicago: Rand McNally.
1983 "French Polynesia: Nuclear Colony." In *Politics in Polynesia,* A. Ali and R. Crocombe, eds., pp.192–226. Suva, Fiji: Institute of Pacific Studies.

Deckker, Paul de, ed.
1983 *The Aggressions of the French at Tahiti and Other Islands of the Pacific* by George Pritchard. Auckland: Auckland University Press and Oxford University Press.

DeWalt, Billie
1975 "Inequalities in Wealth, Adoption of Technology, and Production in a Mexican Ejido." *American Ethnologist* 2:149–168.

Ellis, William
1831 *Polynesian Researches.* 4 vols. London: Fisher and Son.

Ember, Carol
1983 "The Relative Decline of Women's Contribution to Agriculture with Intensification." *American Anthropologist* 85 (2): 285–304.

Epstein, Scarlett
1962 *Economic Development and Social Change in South India.* Manchester: Manchester University Press.

Etienne, M., and E. Leacock
1980 *Women and Colonization: Anthropological Perspectives.* Cambridge, Mass.: J. F. Bergin.

Europa World Yearbook
1985 "French Overseas Territories: French Polynesia." Vol. 2, pp. 1666–1669. London: Europa Publications.
1989 "French Overseas Territories: French Polynesia." Vol. 1, pp. 1071–1075. London: Europa Publications.

Fernandez-Kelley, Maria
1981 "The Sexual Division of Labor, Development, and Women's Status." *Current Anthropology* 22 (4): 414–419.

Finney, Ben
1973 *Polynesian Peasants and Proletarians.* Cambridge, Mass.: Schenkman.

Finney, Ben, and R. A. Watson, eds.
1975 *A New Kind of Sugar: Tourism in the Pacific.* Honolulu: East-West Center.

Firth, Raymond
1946 *Malay Fishermen: Their Peasant Economy.* London: Routledge and Kegan Paul.

Fisk, E. K., and R. T. Shand
1969 "The Early Stages of Development in a Primitive Economy: Evolution from Subsistence to Trade and Specialization." In *Subsistence Agriculture and Economic Development,* C. Wharton, ed., pp. 257–274. Chicago: Aldine.

Forman, Charles
1988 "The Impact of Colonial Policy on the Churches of Tahiti and New Caledonia." *International Review of Mission* 77:12–21.

Frank, Andre Gunder
1966 "The Development of Underdevelopment." *Monthly Review* 18:17–31.

Friedl, Ernestine
     1988 "Society and Sex Roles." In *Anthropology 88/89,* E. Angeloni, ed., pp. 164–
          168. Guildford, Conn.: Dushkin.
Gailey, Christine W.
     1987 *Kinship to Kingship: Gender Hierarchy and State Formation in the Tongan
          Islands.* Austin: University of Texas Press.
Gibbon, P., and M. Neocosmos
     1985 "Some Problems in the Political Economy of 'African Socialism.'" In
          Contradictions in Accumulation in Africa, H. Bernstein and B. Campbell, eds.,
          pp. 153–206. Beverly Hills: Sage.
Goldman, Irving
     1970 *Ancient Polynesian Society.* Chicago: University of Chicago Press.
Graves, N., and T. Graves
     1974 "Adaptive Strategies in Urban Migration." *Annual Review of Anthropology*
          3:117–151.
Gunson, Niel
     1964 "Great Women and Friendship Contract Rites in Pre-Christian Tahiti."
          Journal of the Polynesian Society 73 (1): 53–69.
Hanson, F. Allan
     1970 *Rapan Lifeways: Society and History on a Polynesian Island.* Boston: Little,
          Brown.
     1973 "Political Change in Tahiti and Samoa: An Exercise in Experimental
          Anthropology." *Ethnology* 12 (1): 1–13.
     1982 "Female Pollution in Polynesia." *Journal of the Polynesian Society* 91:335–
          381.
Henningham, Stephen
     1989a "Keeping the Tricolor Flying: The French Pacific into the 1990s." *The
          Contemporary Pacific* 1 (1 & 2): 97–132.
     1989b "French Spending in the South Pacific." *Pacific Economic Bulletin* 4 (2):
          31–38.
     1992 *France and the South Pacific: A Contemporary History.* Honolulu:
          University of Hawaii Press.
Henry, Teuira
     1928 *Ancient Tahiti.* Bulletin no. 48. Honolulu: Bernice P. Bishop Museum.
Hooper, Antony
     1985 "Tahitian Healing." In *Healing Practices in the South Pacific,* C. Parsons,
          ed., pp. 158–198. Laie, Hawaii: Institute for Polynesian Studies.
Howard, A., and R. Borofsky, eds.
     1989 *Developments in Polynesian Ethnology.* Honolulu: University of Hawaii
          Press.
Howard, A., and J. Kirkpatrick
     1989 "Social Organization." In *Developments in Polynesian Ethnology,* A.
          Howard and R. Borofsky, eds., pp. 47–94. Honolulu: University of Hawaii
          Press.
INSEE (Institut National de la Statistique et des Études Économiques)
     1973 *Rencensement de 1971.* Papeete, Tahiti: Service du Plan.
Institut Territorial de la Statistique (ITSTAT)
     1991 Resultats du Rencensement Général de la Population de la Polynésie
          Française (1988). Papeete: ITSTAT.
Johnson, Allan
     1971 *Sharecroppers of the Sertao: Economics and Dependence on a Brazilian
          Plantation.* Stanford: Stanford University Press.

Jolly, M., and M. Macintyre, eds.
1989 *Family and Gender in the Pacific: Domestic Contradictions and the Colonial Impact*. Cambridge: Cambridge University Press.

Jones, Anna Laura
1991 "Contemporary Folk Art in French Polynesia." Ph.D. diss., Stanford University.

Joralemon (Lockwood), Victoria
1983a "Agricultural Development and Socioeconomic Change on Tubuai, French Polynesia." PhD. diss., University of California, Los Angeles.
1983b "Collective Land Tenure and Agricultural Development: A Polynesian Case." *Human Organization* 42 (2): 95–105.
1986 "Development and Inequity: The Case of Tubuai, a Welfare Economy in Rural French Polynesia." *Human Organization* 45 (4): 283–295.

Kay, G.
1975 *Development and Underdevelopment*. London: Macmillan.

Kiste, Robert
1993 "New Political Statuses in American Micronesia." In *Contemporary Pacific Societies: Studies in Development and Change*, V. Lockwood et al., eds., pp. 67–80. Englewood Cliffs, N.J.: Prentice-Hall.

Kung, Lydia
1976 "Factory Work and Women in Taiwan: Changes in Self-Image and Status." *Signs* 2:35–58.

Langevin, Christine
1990 *Tahitiennes de la Tradition à L'Intégration Culturelle*. Paris: Éditions l'Harmattan.

Langevin-Duval, Christine
1979 "Condition et Statut des Femmes dans L'Ancienne Société Maohi (Îles de la Société)." *Journal de la Société des Océanistes* 35 (64): 185–194.
1980 "Traditions et Changements Culturels Chez les Femmes Tahitiennes." *Bulletin de la Société des Études Océaniennes* 17 (11): 577–582.

Levin, Paula
1978 "Students and Teachers on Tubuai: A Cultural Analysis of Polynesian Classroom Interaction." Ph.D. diss., University of California, San Diego.

Levin, P., and V. Lockwood
1984 "The Contribution of Western Education to Rural Underdevelopment on Tubuai, French Polynesia." Paper presented at the annual meeting of the American Anthropological Association, Denver.

Levy, Robert
1973 *Tahitians: Mind and Experience in the Society Islands*. Chicago: University of Chicago Press.

Lingenfelter, Sherwood
1977 "Socioeconomic Change in Oceania." *Oceania* 48 (2): 102–120.

Linnekin, Jocelyn
1986 "Women as Exchangers in Pre-Contact Hawai'i?" Paper presented at the annual meeting of the American Anthropological Association, Philadelphia.
1990 *Sacred Queens and Women of Consequence: Rank, Gender and Colonialism in the Hawaiian Islands*. Ann Arbor: University of Michigan Press.

Lockwood (Joralemon), Victoria
1988a "Capitalist Development and the Socioeconomic Position of Tahitian Peasant Women." *Journal of Anthropological Research* 44 (3): 263–285.
1988b "Development, French Neocolonialism, and the Structure of the Tubuai Economy." *Oceania* 58 (3): 176–192.

1989 "Tubuai Women Potato Planters and the Political Economy of Intra-Household Gender Relations." In *The Household Economy: Reconsidering the Domestic Mode of Production*, R. Wilk, ed., pp. 197–229. Boulder: Westview Press.

1990 "Development and Return Migration to Rural French Polynesia." *International Migration Review* 24 (2): 347–371.

1993 "Welfare State Colonialism in Rural French Polynesia." In *Contemporary Pacific Societies: Studies in Development and Change*, V. Lockwood, et al., eds., pp. 81–97. Englewood Cliffs, N.J.: Prentice-Hall.

Long, Norman

1982 *An Introduction to the Sociology of Rural Development.* Boulder: Westview Press.

Marcus, G., and M. Fischer

1986 *Anthropology as Cultural Critique.* Chicago: University of Chicago Press.

Marshall, Donald

1961 *Ra'ivavae: An Expedition to the Most Fascinating and Mysterious Island in Polynesia.* New York: Doubleday.

Marx, Karl

1969 *Theories of Surplus Value,* Part I. Moscow: Progress.

Maude, H. E.

1959 "The Tahitian Pork Trade." *Journal de la Société des Océanistes* 15:55–95.

McHenry, Donald

1975 *Micronesia: Trust Betrayed.* New York and Washington: Carnegie Endowment for International Peace.

Mies, Maria

1982 "The Dynamics of the Sexual Division of Labor and the Integration of Rural Women into the World Market." In *Women and Development: The Sexual Division of Labor in Rural Societies,* L. Beneria, ed., pp. 1–28. New York: Praeger.

Mintz, Sidney

1977 "The So-called World System: Local Initiative and Local Response." *Dialectical Anthropology* 2:253–270.

Mukhopadhyay, C., and P. Higgins

1988 "Anthropological Studies of Womens' Status Revisited: 1977–1987." *Annual Review of Anthropology* 17:461–495.

Nash, June

1977 "Women and Development: Dependency and Exploitation." *Development and Change* 8:161–182.

1981 "Ethnographic Aspects of the World Capitalist System." *Annual Review of Anthropology* 10:393–423.

Newbury, Colin

1980 *Tahiti Nui: Change and Survival in French Polynesia 1776–1945.* Honolulu: University of Hawaii Press.

Oliver, Douglas

1961 *The Pacific Islands.* Honolulu: University of Hawaii Press.

1974 *Ancient Tahitian Society.* 3 vols. Honolulu: University of Hawaii Press.

1981 *Two Tahitian Villages: A Study in Comparison.* Honolulu: Institute for Polynesian Studies.

1989 *Oceania: The Native Cultures of Australia and the Pacific Islands.* 2 vols. Honolulu: University of Hawaii Press.

Ortner, Sherry

1981 "Gender and Sexuality in Hierarchical Societies: The Case of Polynesia and Some Comparative Implications." In *Sexual Meanings: The Cultural*

Construction of Gender and Sexuality, S. Ortner and H. Whitehead, eds., pp. 359–409. Cambridge: Cambridge University Press.

Pacific Islands Monthly
1980 "Independence Not On." *Pacific Islands Monthly* 51 (July–December): 23.

Panoff, Michel
1962 "Mariage de Naissance dans Trois Districts de Polynésie Française." *Bulletin de la Société d'Études Océaniennes* 12 (3): 129–135.
1970 *La Terre et l'Organization Sociale en Polynésie Française.* Paris: Payot.
1971 "The Society Islands: Confusion from Compulsive Logic." In *Land Tenure in the Pacific,* R. Crocombe, ed., pp. 43–59. Melbourne: Oxford University Press.

Pelto, P., and G. Pelto
1973 *The Snowmobile Revolution: Technology and Social Change in the Arctic.* Menlo Park, Calif.: Cummings.

Peoples, James
1978 "Dependence in a Micronesian Economy." *American Ethnologist* 5 (3): 535–552.
1986 *Island in Trust: Culture Change and Dependence in a Micronesian Economy.* Boulder: Westview Press.

Perrin, Yves
1978 "Towards the Development of Adapted Educational Programs in Tubuai." Ph.D. diss., Columbia University.

Petersen, Glenn
1993 "Some Pohnpei Strategies for Economic Suvival." In *Contemporary Pacific Societies: Studies in Development and Change.* V. Lockwood et al., eds., pp. 185–196. Englewood Cliffs, N.J.: Prentice Hall.

Pollock, Nancy
1978 "Takapoto: La Prosperité, Retour aux Îles." *Journal de la Société des Océanistes* 34 (60): 133–135.
1979 "Économie des Atolls." *Bulletin de la Société des Océanistes* 17 (8): 463–476.

Ravault, François
1979 *Le Régime Foncier de la Polynésie Française.* Centre ORSTOM de Papeete. Paris: Office de la Recherche Scientifique et Technique d'Outre-Mer.

Reiter, Rayna
1975 "Men and Women in the South of France: Public and Private Domains." In *Toward an Anthropology of Women,* Rayna Rapp, ed., pp. 252–282. New York: Monthly Review Press.

Ringon, Gérard
1971 "Vaitapu, un Quartier de Migrants dans la Zone Urbaine de Tahiti." *Journal de la Société des Océanistes* 27:235–247.

Robertson, George
1948 *The Discovery of Tahiti.* Edited by Hugh Carrington. London: The Hakluyt Society.

Robineau, Claude
1977 "Takapoto: Étude Socioéconomique." *Journal de la Société des Océanistes* 54–55:3–37.

Rodman, Margaret
1986 "Constraining Capitalism: Contradictions in Fisheries Development in Vanuatu." Paper presented at the annual meeting of the American Anthropological Association, Philadelphia.
1993 "Keeping Options Open: Copra and Fish in Rural Vanuatu." In *Contemporary Pacific Societies: Studies in Development and Change,* V.

Lockwood, et al., eds., pp. 171–184. Englewood Cliffs, N.J.: Prentice-Hall.

Roseberry, William
1976 "Rent, Differentiation and the Development of Capitalism Among Peasants." *American Anthropologist* 78:45–58.
1989 "Peasants and the World." In *Economic Anthropology,* S. Plattner, ed., pp. 108–126. Stanford: Stanford University Press.

Sacks, Karen
1974 "Engels Revisited: Women, the Organization of Production and Private Property." In *Woman, Culture and Society.* M. Rosaldo and L. Lamphere, eds., pp. 207–222. Stanford: Stanford University Press.
1979 *Sisters and Wives.* Westport, Conn.: Greenwood Press.

Sahlins, Marshall
1958 *Social Stratification in Polynesia.* Seattle: University of Washington Press.

Sanday, Peggy
1974 "Female Status in the Public Domain." In *Woman, Culture and Society,* M. Rosaldo and L. Lamphere, eds., pp. 189–206. Stanford: Stanford University Press.

Schlegel, Alice
1977 *Sexual Stratification: A Cross-Cultural View.* New York: Columbia University Press.

Schuster, Ilsa
1982 "Recent Research on Women in Development." *Journal of Development Studies* 18 (4): 511–535.

SER (Service de l'Économie Rurale, Polynésie Française)
1960–1965, 1968, 1969, 1971, 1972, 1974, 1975, 1977, 1979, 1980–1987 Rapports Annuels, Secteur Agricole des Australes, Polynésie Française.
1975 *Sixième Plan de Développement Économique et Sociale.* Publication du Gouvernement, Papeete, Tahiti.
1977b *Bulletin Statistiques Agricoles* no. 6, Papeete, Tahiti: Service du Plan, Polynésie Française

Sexton, Lorraine
1993 "Pigs, Pearlshells, and 'Women's Work': Collective Response to Change in Highland Papua New Guinea." In *Contemporary Pacific Societies: Studies in Development and Change.* V. Lockwood et al., eds., pp. 117–134. Englewood Cliffs, N.J.: Prentice Hall.

Shankman, Paul
1976 *Migration and Underdevelopment: The Case of Western Samoa.* Boulder: Westview Press.

Shore, Bradd
1989 "Mana and Tapu." In *Developments in Polynesian Ethnology,* A. Howard and R. Borofsky, eds., pp. 137–174. Honolulu: University of Hawaii Press.

Smith, Carol
1984 "Forms of Production in Practice." *Journal of Peasant Studies* 11:200–221.

Smith, Courtland
1980 "Community Wealth Concentration: Comparisons in General Evolution and Development." *Economic Development and Cultural Change* 28:810–818.

Spoehr, A.
1969 "Port Town and Hinterland in the Pacific Islands." *American Anthropologist* 62:586–592.

Stoler, Ann
1977 "Class Structure and Female Autonomy in Rural Java." *Signs* 3:74–89.

Tagupa, W.
  1976 "France, French Polynesia, and the South Pacific in the Nuclear Age." In *Oceania and Beyond: Essays on the Pacific Since 1945*, F. King, ed., pp. 200–215. Westport, Conn.: Greenwood Press.
Tercinier, G.
  1962 *Rapport de Tournée Pédologique aux Îles Australes*. Institut Français d'Océanie, Section de Pédologie, Nouvelle Calédonie. Paris: Office de la Recherche Scientifique et Technique d'Outre-Mer (ORSTOM).
Thomas, Nicholas
  1987 "Complementarity and History: Misrecognizing Gender in the Pacific." *Oceania* 57 (4): 261–270.
Thompson, V., and R. Adloff
  1971 *The French Pacific Islands: French Polynesia and New Caledonia*. Berkeley: University of California Press.
Turnbull, John
  1813 *A Voyage Round the World in the Years 1800 . . . 1804, in Which the Author Visited Madeira, the Brazils, Cape of Good Hope, the English Settlements of Botany Bay and Norfolk Island, and the Principal Islands in the Pacific Ocean, with a Continuation of Their History to the Present Period*. 2d ed. London: A. Maxwell.
Verin, Paul
  1964 "Notes Socioéconomiques sur l'Île de Rurutu." *Cahiers de l'Institut de Science Appliquée* 7.
Wallerstein, Immanuel
  1974 *The Modern World System*. Vol. 1. *Capitalist Agriculture and the Origins of the European World Economy in the Sixteenth Century*. New York: Academic Press.
Wharton, Clifton
  1971 "Risk, Uncertainty and the Subsistence Farmer: Technological Innovation and Resistance to Change in a Context of Survival." In *Studies in Economic Anthropology*. G. Dalton, ed., pp. 152–178. Washington, D.C.: American Anthropological Association.
Wolf, Eric
  1982 *Europe and the People Without History*. Berkeley: University of California Press.
Worsley, Peter
  1984 *The Three Worlds: Culture and World Development*. Chicago: University of Chicago Press.

▲

Index

▲

About the Book and Author

As culturally diverse, non-Western communities are drawn into the international division of labor, capitalism takes root in a number of ways. This book describes how capitalism has become a part of the lives of rural Tahitians, starting with the arrival of Westerners to the islands and detailing the nature of the transformation wrought by missionaries, merchants, and French colonizers—a transformation whose pace has accelerated with the islands' rapid modernization and incorporation into the French welfare state.

Lockwood's analysis of the impact of capitalism centers around two major themes in Third World development: the structural changes that take place in non-Western socioeconomic systems as capitalist methods of production overwhelm indigenous economic organization; and the nature of the increasing social, economic, and political subordination of women that accompanies Westernization.

Victoria Lockwood is associate professor of anthropology at Southern Methodist University. She is coeditor (with T. Harding and B. Wallace) of *Contemporary Pacific Societies: Studies in Development and Change.*